MOTHERS WHO KILL
THEIR CHILDREN

MOTHERS WHO KILL THEIR CHILDREN

UNDERSTANDING THE ACTS OF MOMS FROM SUSAN SMITH TO THE "PROM MOM"

Cheryl L. Meyer and Michelle Oberman
with
Kelly White, Michelle Rone, Priya Batra,
and Tara C. Proano

NEW YORK UNIVERSITY PRESS
New York and London

To our mothers, and mothers everywhere,
in homage to the sheer force of will, resilience, and
eternal hope they show in undertaking to love,
in spite of all that stands in their way.

NEW YORK UNIVERSITY PRESS
New York and London

© 2001 by New York University
All rights reserved

Library of Congress Cataloging-in-Publication Data
Meyer, Cheryl L., 1959–
Mothers who kill their children : understanding the acts of moms
from Susan Smith to the "Prom Mom" / Cheryl L. Meyer and
Michelle Oberman ; with Kelly White . . . [et al.].
p.   cm.
Includes bibliographical references and index.
ISBN 0-8147-5643-3 (alk. paper) —
ISBN 0-8147-5644-1 (pbk. : alk. paper)
1. Filicide. 2. Infanticide. 3. Women murderers. 4. Mothers—
Psychology. 5. Mothers—Social conditions.   I. Oberman,
Michelle. II. White, Kelly. III. Title.
HV6542 .M48 2001
364.15'23'0852—dc21   2001002177

New York University Press books are printed on acid-free paper,
and their binding materials are chosen for strength and durability.

Manufactured in the United States of America

10 9 8 7 6 5 4 3

CONTENTS

ACKNOWLEDGMENTS

We would like to thank our partners and our families for their patience and love. Without them, this book might have been written, but it would have lacked a soul. We are also indebted to our coauthors Michelle Rone, Tara Proano, Priya Batra, and Kelly White for their long hours of research and their collaboration through the equally long process of writing and editing. We are grateful to our respective institutions, DePaul University and Wright State University, for generous support during the completion of this project. Finally, we are thankful to our editor, Jennifer Hammer, whose encouragement inspired us along the way to completion.

INTRODUCTION

A Brief Cross-Cultural History of Infanticide

❏

There is every reason to believe that infanticide is as old as human society itself, and that no culture has been immune. Throughout history, the crime of infanticide has reflected specific cultural norms and imperatives. For instance, infanticide was legal throughout the ancient civilizations of Mesopotamia, Greece, and Rome, and was justified on grounds ranging from population control to eugenics to illegitimacy.[1] Archeological evidence suggests that infant sacrifice was commonplace among early peoples, including the Vikings, Irish Celts, Gauls, and Phoenicians.[2]

Historians of infanticide cite a host of factors associated with the incidence of this crime: poverty, overpopulation, laws governing inheritance, customs relating to nonmarital children, religious and/or superstitious beliefs regarding disability, eugenics, and maternal madness.[3] This broad range of explanations for the act of a mother killing her child suggests that infanticide takes quite different forms in different cultures. Indeed, there is no intuitively obvious link between the exposure of disabled or otherwise ill-fated newborns in ancient Greece, for example, and the practice of female infanticide in modern-day India.

Nonetheless, a close examination of the circumstances surrounding infanticide reveals a profound commonality linking these seemingly unrelated crimes. Specifically, infanticide may be seen as a response to the societal construction of and constraints upon mothering. Factors such as poverty, stigma, dowry, and disability are significant because they foretell the impact that an additional baby will have upon a mother, as well as upon her existing family.

Infanticide is not a random, unpredictable crime. Instead, it is deeply imbedded in and is a reflection of the societies in which it occurs. The crime of infanticide is committed by mothers who cannot parent their child under the circumstances dictated by their unique position in place and time. These circumstances vary, but the extent to which infanticide is a reflection of the norms governing motherhood is a constant that links seemingly disparate crimes.

Nonetheless, even a cursory survey of cases involving women who kill their children reveals enormous variation in the circumstances surrounding these crimes. However, there is very little systematic research that identifies the patterns associated with such killings. This book sets out to identify clear distinctions among the cases of contemporary women who kill their children, shedding light on why some women commit such acts and what intervention strategies might be helpful in preventing the deaths of other children in the future.

We begin with a historical survey, for it is our belief that if we are to make sense of the persistence of infanticide in contemporary society we must understand the manner in which cultural norms have shaped this crime throughout history. Toward that end, this chapter provides a brief chronological review of the sociocultural imperatives underlying the crime of infanticide in various cultures. We do not seek to provide a comprehensive record of the crime of infanticide. Rather, we wish to illustrate the intricate relationship between a society's construction of parenthood and mothering, and its experience of infanticide.

Ancient Cultures

Anthropologists maintain that prehistoric societies routinely practiced infanticide. The killing of newborns was a means of minimizing the strain on societies with limited resources. Thus, according to anthropologists, disabled or sickly children were particularly at risk of infanticide, as were female children who were viewed as a source of future population growth.[4] Over time, civilizations emerged. An examination of their histories reveals the cultural norms that shaped their varying practices of infanticide. Several civilizations have particularly well-documented histories of infanticide, which illustrate how the prevalence of infanticide may be driven by the sociocultural construction of motherhood.

Greco-Roman Civilization

The earliest mention of infanticide in recorded history relates to disabled newborns, and was committed almost exclusively by fathers rather than mothers. Records from the Babylonian and Chaldean civilizations, dating from approximately 4000 to 2000 B.C., refer to disabled newborns as signs or omens from the gods and prescribe the manner of interpreting and responding to these infants' births. Interestingly, these societies saw disabled children as omens of good or bad things to come, but they did not necessarily kill them.[5] However, by the time of the Greek city-states, the killing of both disabled and able-bodied infants was commonplace. Ancient Greco-Roman literature is replete with references to the exposure of unwanted newborns, and the writings of Plato, Seneca, and Pliny all refer to the practice. Generally, exposure was viewed as a means of population control, undertaken with explicit eugenic overtones. For instance, the militaristic nature of Sparta witnessed the routine exposure of all infants, male and female, thought unlikely to make good soldiers or healthy citizens. Parents of deformed or small newborns were ordered to take their offspring to a mountain or other exposed area and leave them there overnight. If they were still alive in the morning, they were permitted to live.[6]

Under Roman law fathers exercised absolute rule and the state had no jurisdiction over domestic affairs. Thus, "infanticide of bastards, females, or 'excess' children was rarely questioned by the authorities; it was merely part of the *patria potens*, the rights of the head of household."[7] Although Greco-Roman civilization did not experience the extremely limited resources that shaped infanticidal practices in both earlier and later civilizations, many of the leading figures advocated small family size and healthy children. Thus, not only was infanticide not considered a crime, but it may well have been seen as a civic duty.[8]

Early Muslim and Hindu Culture

Prior to the advent of Islam in seventh-century Arabia, men possessed women as they would possess any other property.[9] In marriage, a woman's consent was not needed, and husbands often purchased their wives from the women's fathers.[10] Men also enjoyed the right to divorce women at will without having to provide them with any maintenance, and they had the right to unlimited polygamy.[11] Upon the husband's death, his wives would be considered part of the estate to be passed on to his heirs.[12] As a result of such ill-treatment of women in pre-Islamic Arabia, female infanticide was a common practice. Women had no hope of inheritance, and were not allowed to legally possess or to alienate their belongings.[13] As a result, they were completely dependent upon their male relatives. To spare their child a life of misery, mothers frequently disposed of their female babies.

Theoretically speaking, the advent of Islam reduced the infanticide rate by elevating the status of women and providing them with an independent legal status.[14] Marriage was to be a contract between a man and a woman, and the marriage gift was to be paid directly to the bride, not to her father.[15] The woman's consent was required, and if there was any coercion by relatives, the woman could seek redress from the courts.

Polygamy was limited to a maximum of four wives, permissible only if it was possible to treat all of them equally.[16] Women were allowed to participate in divorce proceedings and could receive maintenance after divorce. The practice of inheriting a dead man's widow or widows was abolished, as was the practice of female infanticide.[17]

Nonetheless, there is little reason to believe that the practice of female infanticide disappeared. Indeed, over the course of centuries, the Muslim dowry system evolved into such an oppressive institution that even today it constitutes a powerful explanation for the persistence of female infanticide. The shift in dowry practices coincided with the Muslim invasion of India in the thirteenth and fourteenth centuries, and the subsequent blending of Muslim and Hindu cultures. Before the Muslim invasion, a Hindu father commonly gave his new son-in-law a gift for the purpose of starting a new life with his daughter.[18] When the Muslims invaded, the downturn in economic conditions increased the difficulty of finding a bridegroom of sound economic and social standing, and parents of daughters found themselves bidding on the bridegroom to avoid the risk of an unsuitable match.[19] Eventually, at least in India, dowry became a mechanism for extortion, as the prospective groom's family could demand everything a woman's family possessed.

As a result, even in contemporary Indian culture, the birth of a daughter triggers the pressure of saving a suitable dowry. The financial value of the dowry symbolizes the social status of both the bride's and the groom's families, and becomes the mechanism through which the two families demonstrate their wealth and status.[20] Therefore, if a family cannot provide a suitable dowry it risks social ostracism. Among poor rural families, the persistence of female infanticide is attributable to precisely this fear.[21]

Traditional Chinese Culture

Traditional Chinese culture demonstrated a powerful preference for sons, accompanied by a long history of female infanticide. The culture of son-preference grew out of the low position women occupy under the traditional Confucian hierarchical system.[22] This philosophy is demonstrated by the "three bonds" of the family: loyalty on the part of the subject to the ruler, filial obedience, and chastity (on the part of the wife only).[23] The philosophy also specified three additional forms of obedience required of women: obey the father, the husband, and the son. Women who did not follow these obedience laws were subject to divorce, penal sentences, or worse.[24] Female children were considered to be less valuable than males, as they could not make offerings to the family's ancestral sacrifice, could not glorify the family name by taking public office, and could not continue the family line.[25] As such, daughters from both poor and rich families were vulnerable to infanticide.[26]

During the Qing Dynasty of the eighteenth and nineteenth centuries, wealthy families adopted the practice of giving a dowry to the groom's family upon the marriage of a daughter. This enhanced the preference for sons among wealthy families, and caused a shocking increase in female infanticide among dynastic families. One source estimates that a full 10 percent of daughters born into Qing Dynasty families were killed at birth.[27]

The strong desire to bear a son has continued under communist rule. The communist revolution did not alter traditional laws mandating that property pass through the male line, or customary norms dictating that newly married couples live with and care for the husband's parents.[28] A son is considered a necessity, in that he will support his parents in old age and will carry on the family line, whereas a daughter represents a net loss. She will require time and money to raise, and will ultimately marry out of the family, thereby cutting off her ties with her parents.[29] In addition, because cultural norms restricted females from engaging in some crucial agricultural activities, sons rather than daughters became prized in the agrarian family labor force.[30]

The issue of son-preference became particularly salient in 1979, when China implemented a one child per family policy in an effort to stem rapid population growth.[31] This policy, which limits families to one child, has triggered a dramatic rise in the abandonment and infanticide of baby girls, as well as a rise in the abortion of female fetuses.[32] In response to this, the Chinese government has attempted to reform the underlying cultural norms and laws thought to contribute to son-preference. For example, new laws require all children, male and female, to care for their parents. However, the customs favoring sons are so deeply entrenched that to date these changes have had little effect.[33]

Medieval Judeo-Christian Culture

Accompanying the conversion of the Roman Empire to Christianity, in 318 A.D. Constantine declared infanticide to be a crime. Yet all indications are that infanticide remained commonplace throughout early Christian society.[34] The meticulous record keeping of medieval Christian society provides a remarkably rich example of the manner in which cultural norms shaped infanticidal practices.

Infanticide's Prevalence

Although it is difficult to estimate the prevalence of infanticide during any given era, evidence of infanticide during early Christian culture is facilitated by church records of births and deaths, by ecclesiastical law, and by studying demographic records.

For example, evidence of the prevalence of infanticide emerges from occasional references to the crime in medieval handbooks of penance. These describe the sin of *overlaying* a child by lying on top of it and suffocating it.[35] This sin is included in a list of the venial or minor sins, such as failing to be a good samaritan or quarreling with one's wife.[36] From the ninth to the fifteenth centuries, the standard penance for overlaying was three years, one of these on bread and water, while that for the accidental killing of an adult was five years, three of these on bread and water.[37] Scholars consider this casual mention and lenient treatment of infanticide to be evidence of its relatively commonplace nature.[38]

Demographic studies provide a second source for detecting infanticide. Specifically, civil, church, and hospital records yield information about the widespread incidence of infanticide, as well as sex-specific infanticide. For example, in a normal population, 105 to 106 baby boys are born for every 100 girls.[39] During the first year of life, male babies are more vulnerable to infection and disease than are female babies. Therefore, by age one there should be an equal number of boys and girls.[40] As a result, whenever a community reveals sex ratios that diverge significantly from the norm, there is reason to suspect infanticide.[41] Thus, evidence of infanticide is observed in data from fifteenth-century Florence, indicating 114.6 boys per 100 girls, with the ratio jumping to 124.56 boys per 100 girls in upper-class families.[42]

Underlying Causes of Infanticide in Judeo-Christian Europe

Undoubtedly, infanticide in early Judeo-Christian Europe was motivated by many of the same factors that historically have been associated with the crime elsewhere, such as poverty and scarce family resources. However, a profound religious and cultural hostility to nonmarital sex and childbearing became an additional factor associated with infanticide. Although it is impossible to measure the precise extent to which this factor contributed to the rate of infanticide, it is clear from the laws of the era as well as the conclusions of many commentators that "illegitimacy" was widely seen as a motivating factor behind the crime of infanticide.

According to the dictates of the Catholic church, a child born to an unmarried woman was deemed "illegitimate."[43] "As a result of the church's condemnation of non-monogamous relations, Middle Age society virtually disregarded the illegitimate child. Illegitimate children were 'deprived . . . of the ordinary rights of man. . . . Some law books treated them as almost rightless beings, on a par with robbers and thieves.'"[44] Common law protects legitimate children by insuring them the right to their family name, as well as a right to be supported by and to inherit from their families. The nonmarital child was denied all these rights. As a result, they often became the victims of infanticide.[45]

Of course, the children were not the only ones stigmatized by illegitimacy. Regardless of the circumstances of their pregnancy, unmarried mothers suffered considerable social approbation for bearing a child out of wedlock.[46] In addition to social ostracism and public humiliation, a woman could be subjected to prosecution simply for being an unmarried mother. By the start of the seventeenth century, rapid population growth and the intensification of impoverishment led to the perception of growing social disorder.[47] In response to that fear, crimes involving sexual offenses such as bastardy and fornication, which formerly had been tried in church courts and punished by a moderate penance for those convicted, became secularized. The penalties for these crimes were particularly harsh in England. For example, in 1576 Parliament passed a "poor law" which punished the impoverished parents of bastard children. These laws punished by public whipping and/or imprisonment mothers who refused to identify the men who had fathered their illegitimate children.[48]

These laws created an obvious incentive to conceal an illegitimate sexual affair as well as a resulting pregnancy. This incentive was particularly intense for unmarried women whose jobs were jeopardized as a result of pregnancy. For example, the commonplace nature of sexual harassment against women employed as domestic servants fostered a perverse and tragic link between sexuality, pregnancy, and infanticide. As one commentator notes:

> The association between illegitimacy and infanticide in mid and late Victorian England was accentuated by the habit of many employers regarding young unmarried women in service as "fair

game." An illegitimate baby meant almost certain loss of employment and public obloquy, and it is not surprising that secret pregnancies ending in infanticide were not uncommon.[49]

Throughout European society, the link between illegitimacy and infanticide was so widely acknowledged that, to a large extent, infanticide was considered a crime committed exclusively by unmarried women. Many of the earliest statutes outlawing infanticide refer solely to the crime of "bastardy" neonaticide—infanticide committed by an unmarried woman.[50] Even in societies with infanticide laws that governed all citizens, historians speculate that married women who committed infanticide generally avoided punishment. One scholar asserts that in medieval Europe married women so often escaped prosecution for infanticide that they "could kill their infants with relative impunity."[51] The same was not true for unmarried women. For example, one European city's court and prison records from 1513 to 1777 document punishments ranging from burial alive to drowning and decapitation for eighty-seven women, all but four of whom were unmarried, for the crime of infanticide.[52] Interestingly, during the witchcraft inquisition, the crime of infanticide was widely attributed to witches.[53]

Contemporary Infanticide—Twentieth-Century Developments

Until the start of the twentieth century, the Judeo-Christian world seems to have understood infanticide as a crime committed by desperate and/or immoral women. The twentieth century introduced a dramatically new lens through which to view the crime—that of illness. Of course, the persistence of infanticide was not fueled by a sudden epidemic. As before, the crime grew out of poverty and isolation, factors further exacerbated in the twentieth century by demographic shifts in family structure and by a rise in substance abuse. Nonetheless, there is lasting, albeit limited validity to the application of a "medical model" to the crime of infanticide.

The Medicalization of Infanticide

During the late nineteenth century, two French psychiatrists, Esquirol and Marce, posited a causal relationship between pregnancy, childbirth, and subsequent maternal mental disorder.[54] The research, quickly adopted by others, led to a significant change in the way twentieth-century societies viewed infanticide. To varying degrees, people around the world began to associate infanticide with mental illness.

Nowhere was this vision more powerfully embraced than in England, where the infanticide statutes of 1922 and 1938 recognized infanticide as a distinct form of homicide due to the impact of pregnancy and birth upon the mother's mental status. According to these laws, mothers who can show that they suffered from a postpartum mental disorder generally are charged with manslaughter, rather than murder, and the vast majority of such defendants receive probationary sentences and health-care interventions rather than prison sentences. The British Infanticide Act of 1922 is premised upon the belief that a woman who commits infanticide may do so because "the balance of her mind [i]s disturbed by reason of her not having fully recovered from the effect of giving birth to the child."[55] This statute, which has been replicated in slightly varying forms in at least twenty-two nations around the world, limits the defendant's culpability for the crime of infanticide, providing that the maximum crime with which she can be charged is manslaughter rather than murder.[56]

Americans have been far less sanguine with regard to the adoption of a medical model for understanding infanticide. Thus, there are not general federal or state laws governing infanticide. Nor do American medical experts agree about the nature of postpartum mental disorders and their capacity to cause infanticide.[57] Nonetheless, there is general consensus among medical experts on the symptoms of one specific variation of postpartum disorder known to cause infanticidal fantasies, and in rare cases infanticide itself: postpartum psychosis.

Affecting no more than one or two of every one thousand women who give birth, postpartum psychosis is characterized by a dramatic break with reality, accompanied by "a grossly impaired ability to function, usually because of hallucinations or delusions."[58] One of the primary markers of postpartum psychosis is that women experience delusional fantasies related to their newborns. Most such women report auditory hallucinations in which voices urge them to kill the child.[59] In addition to psychotic hallucinations, women suffering from postpartum psychosis characteristically display other unusual behavioral tendencies. They isolate themselves, stop speaking to others, and often talk to themselves in an agitated fashion. They are severely sleep-deprived and emotionally labile.[60]

Women who kill their infants during an episode of postpartum psychosis tend to manifest these characteristics at an extreme level. For example, consider the case of Sheryl Massip, a California woman who was charged with killing her six-week-old son. At her 1987 murder trial, evidence showed that she threw her son into oncoming traffic, picked him up and carried him to her garage, where she hit him over the head with a blunt object and finally killed him by running him over with her car.[61]

Massip's story is fairly typical of postpartum psychosis-related infanticides. She continued to manifest severely disordered thinking after she killed her child, telling investigators that a black object, who "wasn't really a person," with orange hair and white gloves, had kidnaped the baby.[62] By definition, postpartum psychosis is brief in duration, and even if untreated, symptoms virtually always disappear within several months of onset.[63] Therefore, by the time of her trial Massip was no longer psychotic. The jury found Massip guilty of second-degree murder, and she was jailed. Two months later, the judge overturned the verdict and acquitted Massip on insanity grounds.[64]

Beyond Madness: The Sociocultural Underpinnings of
Twentieth-Century Infanticide

Although Americans have not embraced the medical model for infanticide as fully as have England, Canada, and other nations, the U.S. criminal justice system has accommodated and provided a partial defense to defendants in a small set of cases involving postpartum mental disorders. Nonetheless, the impact of this accommodation upon the entire body of infanticide cases is minimal. Regardless of the extent to which U.S. medical experts and judges are accepting of postpartum psychosis as a disorder and a defense to homicide charges, it is evident that this diagnosis simply does not apply to the vast majority of cases involving mothers who kill their children.

When one gathers hundreds of such cases and pours over them looking for similarities and differences, it becomes evident that neither mental illness nor the excuses of generations past (poverty, illegitimacy, and the like) fully explain the persistence of infanticide into the twenty-first century. Indeed, one might have expected infanticide rates to drop with twentieth-century developments such as effective contraception, legalized abortion, and a greater acceptance of nonmarital childbearing.[65] Yet throughout the course of the twentieth century, infanticide persisted as a crime of desperation.

As has been the case throughout history, infanticide in the twentieth and twenty-first centuries may be understood as a response to the societal construction of and constraints upon mothering. The sociocultural imperatives underlying the contemporary crime of infanticide include the fragmentation of the extended family and ultimately of the nuclear family as well. By the end of the twentieth century, close to 30 percent of all households with children under the age of eighteen were headed by one parent rather than two.[66] Single parenthood in the context of a fragmented community and in the absence of an extended family means that all the tasks of parenting must be borne more or less alone.[67] This scenario is challenging for all, but particularly so for those lacking the

13

inner resources to withstand the enormous pressures of parenting a young child. Among those who are particularly vulnerable as single, isolated parents are those who have survived abusive childhoods. By the end of the twentieth century, social problems such as child abuse and substance abuse became the focus of considerable public concern. It became clear that the legacy of child abuse was long and complex, and that those who had grown up in abusive homes were at risk of replicating the harmful behaviors they had witnessed or experienced as children.[68]

Although it is clear that many survivors of abusive childhoods go on to become perfectly competent parents, there is a growing body of evidence indicating that the majority of parents who *are abusive* were themselves abused as children.[69] Among the personality characteristics observed in survivors of abuse are low self-esteem, poor impulse control, depression, anxiety, and antisocial behavior, including aggression and substance abuse.[70] It is not difficult to envision how these particular characteristics might complicate parenting. By definition, parenting requires tremendous patience, energy, endurance, and maturity. If one combines the preexisting vulnerabilities of a woman who has been abused with the challenges of parenting in socially isolated and economically vulnerable circumstances, the fact that some small number of mothers abuse and even kill their children might be seen as inevitable.[71]

The mentally ill are an equally vulnerable population of parents. Beginning in the 1960s, the United States embarked upon a course known as "deinstitutionalization," which, although originally intended to protect the rights of mentally ill persons, has resulted in a dramatic curtailment of resources for the housing and treatment of this population.[72] At the end of 1968, there were 399,000 patients in state mental hospitals.[73] Within a decade, the hospital population fell by 64 percent to 147,000.[74] Major acceleration in the movement to deinstitutionalize state mental patients began after 1968 in most jurisdictions.[75]

The housing and treatment problems appeared almost immediately. In a rush to capitalize on the availability of federal funds for community mental health centers, states often released patients who were not able to care for themselves.[76] Once these patients were released, community facilities were overwhelmed and lacked the resources to assist those who depended on their services. During this period, single-room occupancy hotels rarely had vacancies "due to the increasing gentrification of the inner cities."[77] This proved detrimental to the mentally ill who not only needed a bed, but also an address where benefit checks could be received.

Part of the problem was that community mental health centers had to be transformed from agencies helping those who wanted brief and temporary counseling (i.e., marriage counseling or stress management) to agencies charged with assisting the chronically mentally ill.[78] This transformation would have required a considerable investment of resources, as the community mental health networks were ill-equipped to handle the mentally ill, let alone the homeless mentally ill.[79] That investment of resources never came. Today, the chronically mentally ill frequently are caught in a vicious cycle. These individuals deteriorate in the community to the point where they are admitted in acute crisis to a hospital, often via the local jail.[80] They are then stabilized on medication in the hospital and released with no discharge planning or aftercare services. Without treatment or community support services, they again degenerate to the point of requiring hospitalization, revolving continuously back and forth between hospitals and the streets.[81] It does not take much imagination to understand how difficult the burdens of parenting would be for this population. For those who suffer from chronic mental illness, parenting in isolation and without access to any meaningful ongoing support may become a prescription for child abuse.

Many of the infanticide deaths that occurred during the latter half of the twentieth century reflect the foregoing confluence of factors. In retrospect, the children's deaths often emerge as inevitable. Consider, for example, the following two cases:

Guinevere Garcia

Guinevere Garcia spent five years on death row in Illinois for the separate crimes of killing her eleven-month-old daughter, and later her abusive husband. Her sentence was commuted to life imprisonment in January 1996.[82] From the time she was six years old, Garcia was raped repeatedly by an older male relative with whom she lived.[83] Her mother, who had also been raped by this man, committed suicide when Garcia was eighteen months old. Garcia began drinking heavily at age eleven. Between ages eleven and nineteen, she suffered numerous traumas, including being gang-raped and being forced into a sham marriage with an undocumented man.

At age nineteen, Garcia gave birth to a daughter, and was struggling to support herself and her daughter by prostitution and nude dancing. By the time her daughter was eleven months old, Garcia became terrified that she would lose custody and that her daughter would be raised in the same home environment to which she and her mother had been subjected. One day, when she was overwhelmed by these fears, she smothered her daughter. The police did not discover the crime until they came to interview Garcia two years later, regarding two fires that had occurred in her apartment building. She told the police that she had set both of the fires, a year apart, on the first and second anniversaries of her daughter's death. Garcia confessed to having killed her daughter, and led the police to the spot where she had buried her daughter's body.

Simone Ayton

A second case illustrating the complex sociocultural underpinnings of twentieth-century infanticide involves Simone Ayton, a mildly retarded, manic-depressive woman with cerebral palsy, who lived alone with her eight-month-old son.[84] Ayton received no financial or emotional support from the baby's father or from her family. When her son was twenty-two days old, Ayton brought him to a community hospital, where he was diagnosed as suffering from dehydration and fever. She claimed he would not eat because he did not like her. This triggered a custody hearing, at which the judge ordered the child placed in foster care based upon his finding that Ayton was "emotionally unable to care for the child."

Ayton spent the next seven months working to meet the state's requirements for reunification with her child. She ultimately earned the support of her caseworkers, and her child was returned to her custody. Less than a week later, Ayton's son was dead. Ayton first told authorities that she had been bathing her son when he slipped from her arms and fell into the water. Later she admitted to a detective that she was frustrated with the child's crying and so she held him under the water until he stopped struggling.

Both these cases involved mothers who suffered from some degree of mental trauma, yet neither case can be explained or excused on the basis of postpartum mental illness alone. Instead, sociocultural and economic influences such as disability, substance abuse, and unresolved trauma combined with the pressures associated with being the sole caretaker for an infant prefigure the infants' deaths. This general pattern was reflected in a remarkable number of twentieth-century infanticide cases.

Ironically, this pattern is eclipsed by the manner in which most societies regard infanticide. Most contemporary societies view infanticide as a uniform crime. It may be treated either as a manifestation of illness or as a manifestation of evil, yet little attention is paid to the manner in which these cases are similar to one another, and to the manner in which they are different.

It is the goal of this book to clarify the genesis of these cases in contemporary U.S. culture, illustrating both the similarities and differences among the women who commit infanticide. We undertook this process by approaching each case on its own terms, looking at it from the mother's perspective and asking and attempting to answer the question,

"Why did she do it?" This process yielded a surprisingly obvious set of responses, and the cases easily sorted themselves out into the five categories discussed in this book. By providing a contextual understanding of the reasons why women may be moved to kill their children, we hope to make possible more meaningful policies, well-tailored intervention strategies, and more comprehensive evaluations of these cases when they arise.

I

PREVIOUS ATTEMPTS TO UNDERSTAND WHY MOTHERS KILL THEIR CHILDREN

❏

There is a morbid curiosity in the United States relating to mothers killing their children. This fascination becomes evident when cases such as those of Susan Smith, Amy Grossberg, and Melissa Drexler (aka the "prom Mom") become a media frenzy. On an anecdotal level, every researcher on this project can relate numerous stories about how an otherwise dull conversation became lively when people learned the topic of our research. In those conversations people wanted to hear cases, but more often wanted to discuss explanations. Generally they did not want to hear our research-driven conclusions, but rather to present their own, often ill-informed explanations and opinions. These may have related to their beliefs regarding the inflated use of the insanity defense (in fact applied in only a very small percentage of cases) or their theories about what "kind" of mother could kill her child.

On a scholarly level, most researchers have continually referred to mothers who kill their children as a homogeneous group with little differentiation among the women. However, even a cursory review of cases makes it clear that there are at least two groups which can be distinguished from each other: mothers who commit neonaticide,[1] killing their newborns, and mothers who commit other forms of filicide, killing their child.[2] For example, Melissa Drexler, who disposed of her newborn baby in a restroom trash bin at her high school prom, is very different from Susan Smith, who drowned her fourteen-month-old and two-year-old by driving her car into a lake. In obvious ways, their actions, demographics, and reactions were different. Prevention and intervention strategies should obviously differ for a teenage mother who committed neonaticide and a mother who killed her two children and fabricated a story about their whereabouts.[3]

A typology is needed so that people can begin to understand the many reasons for the occurrence of infanticide. This typology could assist educators in targeting more effective prevention strategies, practitioners in providing more focused intervention, law enforcement officers in their investigations, and legislators in creating more meaningful policy. Moreover, the general public, whose loved ones may be at risk, who as taxpayers pay for consequences of maternal filicide, and who influence public policy, may benefit on many levels from greater understanding of this tragedy. To begin, we will review attempts at previous typologies and their shortcomings.

Previous Attempts at Classification

In 1969 and 1970, psychiatrist Philip Resnick provided a classification system based on apparent motive.[4] As Resnick's was the first attempt at a typology and is the most widely noted, it is important to discuss it here in detail. However, it is also important to understand at the outset that his research methodology was relatively weak and not specifically focused on women, and is now largely outdated.

Resnick based his system on cases of both paternal and maternal filicide. He reviewed the world literature on child murder from 1751 to

1968 and found relevant articles in thirteen languages. From that literature, he amassed 131 case reports of filicide and 34 case reports of neonaticides in which the mother had acted alone. "The cases are reported in varying detail from mental hospitals, psychiatrists in practice, prison psychiatrists, and a coroner's office. . . . Although this variation creates difficulties for analysis of data, the problem of small sample size is eliminated. To illustrate how filicide may be unconsciously multidetermined, two cases treated by the author, including material gathered during sodium amobarbital (Amytal) interviews, will be presented."[5] Resnick identified two general types of cases, filicide and neonaticide. He then divided filicide into five categories, namely, acutely psychotic, altruistic, unwanted child, accidental, and spouse revenge.

Resnick defined acutely psychotic as parents who killed under the influence of hallucinations, epilepsy, or delusions. The category of altruistic filicide was divided into that associated with suicide and that intended to relieve suffering. In the former subcategory, suicidal parents indicated they could not abandon their child when they killed themselves. In the second subcategory, the filicide represented euthanasia aimed at eliminating the child's real or imagined suffering. In Resnick's third category, that of unwanted child, the parent murdered the child because s/he did not want the child. For mothers, Resnick indicated the child may have represented an impediment to a new relationship or been the product of illegitimacy. The accidental filicide category represented unintentional deaths that were generally the result of abuse. Finally, Resnick's last category, spouse revenge, was defined as parents who kill children in an attempt to make their spouse suffer.

Some of Resnick's filicide categories have little applicability to women. For example, he offered no evidence to support a spousal revenge motive in women.[6] Moreover, "it is in practice extremely difficult to be sure that revenge was the real or the only motivation; to find that there is currently a quarrel with the spouse is not sufficient reason for supposing that revenge is predominant. Often in such circumstances other motivations, especially inability to bear the prospect of deprivation, loss of love, or loss of status, are equally if not more prominent."[7] In addition, although Resnick found that the majority of filicidal women fit under the altruistic murder category, only the murder/suicide subcategory has received subsequent research support, not the euthanasia category.[8] Some have questioned the existence of an altruistic motivation altogether: "'Realistic altruism' in fact means 'mercy-killing,' and to combine this with such an entirely different condition as killing under the influence of a delusional psychosis seems inappropriate."[9]

Regarding neonaticide, Resnick responded to what he believed was a prior overemphasis on the social context of neonaticide by focusing on psychiatric factors:

> Most neonaticides are carried out simply because the child is not wanted. Reasons for neonaticide include extramarital paternity, rape, and seeing the child as an obstacle to parental ambition. However, illegitimacy, with its social stigma, is the most common motive.
>
> The unmarried murderesses fall into two groups. In the first group are young, immature, passive women who submit to, rather than initiate, sexual relations. They often deny their pregnancy, and premeditation is rare. The women in the second group have strong instinctual drives and little ethical restraint. They tend to be older, more callous, and are often promiscuous. It is speculated that unresolved oedipal feelings may contribute to some neonaticides that have previously been attributed to entirely sociologic factors.[10]

Interestingly, despite his attempts to find psychoanalytic causes for infanticide, even Resnick identifies the social stigma of pregnancy outside marriage as the most common motive for neonaticide. However, approaching infanticide from a psychoanalytic perspective and focusing on intrapsychic or psychological causes creates a general problem for Resnick's classification systems. Resnick indicated that two-thirds of the filicidal group of women were psychotic,[11] a finding that receives little empirical support elsewhere. This focus on the individual is relatively outdated, given the current emphasis on the importance of environmental, cultural, and social factors in the development of personality and psychopathology.[12] In addition, there is a waning interest in orthodox Freudian psychoanalysis,[13] especially given the lack of sensitivity to women's issues inherent in purely psychoanalytic approaches. As psychologist P. D. Scott has argued, Resnick's system

> relies heavily on motivation which is always highly suggestive and often over-determined, or defensive. . . . Direct observation of murderers suggest[s] that the majority commit the offense when their higher controls of discretion, reason, sympathy, and self-criticism are more or less in abeyance, and when they are in fact acting at so primitive a level that such sophisticated motives as revenge and altruism may be quite inappropriate. Passion and need are commonly accepted as precursors of, or even mitigating factors for, crime, but the importance of long-continued states of indecision and suspense are often overlooked. Yet it is stress of this continuing sort which is most likely to undermine defences [sic], and to uncover actions which are more familiar to ethologists [sic] than to psychopathologists. Inexplicable murders and destruction brought about in this way tend to be wrongly diagnosed "depression" or else a new label such as "catathymic crisis" or "autonomous affective crisis" is invented, often with complicated psychodynamic interpretations of what may simply be facilitation of primitive reactions by *prolonged* frustration and indecision.[14]

There are other problems with Resnick's classification system as well. Many of the cases upon which Resnick's system was founded were quite old, and came from various sources, languages, and cultures. These sources may not apply to infanticide in the United States. Resnick indicates that less common methods of neonaticide "include dismemberment, burning, acid, lye, throwing to pigs, and burying alive."[15] Some of these methods represent cultural or temporal distinctions that are not relevant to a contemporary U.S. context.

Although Resnick's system represented a first attempt at a typology, it was formulated in the 1960s and few would argue that women's societal status and roles have remained constant since that time. In general, norms related to sexuality, illegitimacy, and reproductive rights have undergone major transformations. For example, the social stigma associated with unwed mothering has clearly decreased since 1969. Married couples have been guaranteed the right to be free from criminal prosecution for using contraceptives since 1965[16] and this right was extended to unmarried couples in 1972.[17] Eventually the right to a legal, safe abortion was provided in 1973.[18] (The relationship between abortion and infanticide has been considered elsewhere in this book.) In recent decades, scholars have posited alternatives to Resnick's system.

In 1973, Scott,[19] a British forensic psychiatrist, developed a new system of classification of parental filicide that, like Resnick's system, was not specific to women. His categories included elimination of an unwanted child (by assault or neglect), mercy killing, gross mental pathology, stimulus arising outside the victim (e.g., revenge), and the victim constituting the stimulus (e.g., exasperation). d'Orban, another British forensic psychiatrist, later refined Scott's categories to be specific to women.[20] His six groups included mothers who batter, mentally ill mothers, those who commit neonaticide, retaliating women, those with unwanted children, and those who kill out of mercy. With battering mothers, the filicide occurred due to an impulsive act characterized by loss of temper and the immediate stimulus arose from the victim. Mentally ill mothers included those who suffered from psychosis, depression, and personality disorders. Neonaticides and retaliating women were classified the same way as Resnick had done. Passive neglect or active aggression killed unwanted children. Mercy killings represented cases in which the victim was really suffering and the mother obtained no secondary gain by the death.

d'Orban reviewed the cases of all women charged with killing or attempting to murder their children who were admitted to Holloway Prison in England from 1970 to 1975. d'Orban's sample consisted of eighty-nine women, forty-one of whom he personally examined. In addition, he reviewed all available records including depositions, psychiatric histories, and probation officer, police, and relative reports. Overall, d'Orban found that the women suffered from common family, social, and psychiatric stressors such as severe marital discord with a husband or cohabitee, housing problems, financial difficulties, and youthful parenting. Some of these stressors were more prevalent among certain categories. d'Orban was also the first to note the high percentage of firstborn or only children that become victims. Baker[21] later found the same pattern. d'Orban found very little support for the mercy killing category (only one out of eighty-nine women fell into this category) and slight support for the retaliatory category (11 percent). Forty percent of mothers were classified as battering, 27 percent as mentally ill, 12 percent as neonaticides, and 9 percent as mothers of unwanted children.

Bourget and Bradford provided another classification of homicidal parents in 1990.[22] They defined five major categories: pathological filicide (including altruistic motives and homicide/suicide), accidental filicide, retaliating filicide, neonaticide, and paternal filicide. Bourget and Bradford compared the characteristics of thirteen homicidal parents with those of forty-eight homicide offenders whose victim was not their child. Their sample consisted of all cases of child murder referred to a university-based forensic psychiatry service during an eight-year period (1978–1986). There were four males and nine females, and all resided in Canada. Most of their data were obtained through psychological assessment. They found that homicidal parents had been under severe stress in the previous year. In contrast to Resnick, they found little support for their pathological filicide category, which included altruistic motives, but strong support for their accidental filicide category, which included battered child cases. Once again, there was little support for the retaliating filicide category.

In 1991, Baker[23] began to formulate a more comprehensive approach by using a qualitative and semiquantitative study of all officially suspected cases of filicide in Victoria, Australia, between 1978 and 1988. Like Resnick and Bourget and Bradford, Baker included filicidal fathers in her sample in order to conduct a gender analysis. Baker used the Murder Book as her source to identify cases of filicide. The Murder Book, compiled by a researcher employed by the police department in Australia, contains the names of every suspected homicide case that comes to the attention of the police. Entries in the Murder Book include the names and addresses of suspected offenders and the deceased, a brief description of the case and sometimes the findings of the inquest and/or verdict. Baker also examined the Coroner's file index, the Registrar General's files, and records from the Department of Public Prosecutions. Documents she was able to assess through these means included the prosecution brief, the autopsy and toxicologist's report, police records of interviews, coroner's findings, correspondence, the record of investigation into the death, and a transcript of the inquest. Not every document was available on every case but Baker indicated that most files contained between one hundred to more than one thousand pages of material. She collected information on numerous variables including demographics, specifics of the crime and motive, the psychological state of the offender, relationship between offender and victim, dynamics of the household, disposition of cases, and factors associated with neonaticide.

Baker's sample consisted of forty-six cases; of the twenty-five women among them, 24 percent committed neonaticide (no men committed neonaticide). Baker identified six major motives for the filicides, namely, altruism, spouse murder or revenge, jealousy and rejection, unwanted child, discipline-related cases, and self-defense. Three of the motives did not apply to the women in her sample. These motives were: spouse murder or revenge, jealousy and rejection, and self-defense. For women, altruistic motives were slightly more prevalent than discipline-related or unwanted child filicide motives. Suicidal women were only found in the altruistic group. Altruistic motives included mothers killing their children because they saw themselves as the victims of an incestuous rape and/or believed the children would be better off dead.

Interestingly, for one quarter of the women in this category, altruism was combined with the belief that they were uniting their families in death. Baker cautioned that her categories were broad and "motivation is complex and may involve numerous cultural, environmental and psychological factors."[24] Baker is quick to point out the flaws in her study, including biases in reporting and a small sample size. Nevertheless, the comprehensiveness of her approach is impressive.

In 1997, a few years after Baker's original research on the topic, Alder and Baker published a report extending Baker's original data analysis to 1991 and focusing on maternal filicide. There were thirty-two identified incidents of maternal filicide during that time period. Alder and Baker divided the cases into three groupings: filicide and suicide, which comprised eleven of the cases,[25] neonaticide, which made up ten of the cases, and fatal assaults, seven of the cases (four of the cases could not be used in their analyses). Alder and Baker indicated that in general women in the filicide and suicide group were "most often over 30 years of age with two or more young children, who felt that they could no longer cope with the difficult circumstances in which they found themselves and killed themselves and their children whom they believed would be better off dead."[26]

Interestingly, Alder and Baker found the mothers' desire to care for their children reflected in the detailed instructions they left in suicide notes regarding the child's burial and/or the extensive preparation the mothers undertook in order to insure that their homicidal efforts were successful. In general, women in the neonaticidal category feared the repercussions of pregnancy and never came to terms with the pregnancy or birth. In the fatal assault group, the women did not intend to kill the child but generally there was a previous pattern of physical abuse. Alder and Baker found that the women in this category faced a number of difficulties in life, including "financial problems, inadequate housing, dislike of the child, health problems, exhaustion, frustration, depression, isolation and lack of practical support."[27]

Alder and Baker's groupings are based largely on the same sample of cases as were Baker's before. The addition of seven cases to the original research did not reconfigure their groupings considerably but allowed for refinement. Unfortunately, the applicability of their research to women in the United States is relatively unknown. Alder and Baker conclude that "It is apparent from these findings that present conceptualisations of maternal filicide are inadequate: the phenomenon is more diverse and complex than previously identified in most of the research on this topic."[28]

In 1997, Wilczynski constructed what was perhaps the most comprehensive of all the previous classifications.[29] Wilczynski used three samples of child killers—one from England and two from Australia. The English sample consisted of sixty-five case files obtained from the Director of Public Prosecutions in London for the years 1983 and 1984. There were thirty-six females and twenty-nine males in this sample. Files usually contained

> the suspect's interview with the police; witness statements; photographs of the victim and the crime scene; post-mortem report; psychiatric report(s); the "antecedents form" by the police giving brief details of items such as the suspect's finances; the Police Report; the DPP "Murder Note," giving reasons for the decision to prosecute or not, and if so for which offence; correspondence concerning the legal processing of the case; a Brief to Counsel requesting advice; and a note by the Court Clerk concerning the court case and outcome (usually quite brief, but occasionally including a verbatim description of the trial).[30]

Wilczynski's second sample included twenty-two deaths of children between 1989 and 1991 in Australia which were determined by the coroner to be the result of intentional violence. Information was obtained from coroner files and the Department of Community Services (DCS). Files generally included

> a post-mortem report; a P79A Form filled out by the police, providing brief demographic details about the victim and a para-

graph-long summary describing the incident and the investigation; and a form outlining the verdict by the coroner. Some of the coroners' files were also rich sources of other data including for instance inquest transcripts and witness statements by workers involved in the case and friends and relatives of the child and/or family. The DCS files contained a printout of information from the Departments' computerized CIS (Client Information System), and data on the family's history, reasons for DCS contact, and the nature and outcome of DCS inquiries and actions. The content of the DCS files varied considerably in accordance with the nature and length of DCS contact.[31]

Wilczynski's final sample involved twenty-five Australian offenders who were sentenced from 1991 to 1993. These files usually "contained: the police facts as set out by the Officer in Charge; A NSW Police Force Antecedent Form (P16); psychological and/or psychiatric reports and in some cases pre-sentence reports; and sentence remarks at first instance."[32] Clearly, Wilczynski based her classifications on a large amount of data and high number of subjects. She analyzed her data both qualitatively and quantitatively.

Wilczynski identified ten categories of alleged motive. These were: retaliatory killings; jealousy of or rejection by the victim; the unwanted child (including neonaticide); disciplinary; altruistic; psychosis in the parent; Munchausen Syndrome by Proxy; killings secondary to sexual or ritual abuse of the victim or another person; no intent to kill or injure (e.g., neglect); and cases of unknown motive. Wilczynski further subdivided the unwanted child cases into children unwanted and unplanned since the time of conception; older unwanted children; and children wanted by the parent at conception but not after birth. She also subdivided the altruistic cases into "primary altruistic killings" (e.g., mercy killings) and "secondary" altruistic killings (those in which filicide is secondary to depression in the parent).

Wilczynski found that two of her categories exclusively or almost exclusively reflected male motives. These were retaliatory and jealousy/ rejection. Similarly, there were three categories that exclusively or almost exclusively reflected female motives. These were: unwanted child; psychotic parent; and Munchausen Syndrome by Proxy. Disciplinary homicides were more common among men than among women. There was little support in Wilczynski's sample for filicide secondary to sexual or ritual abuse, "primary" altruistic killings, or filicide due to neglect. However, Wilczynski reasoned that the neglect cases may have been absent because no criminal proceedings were initiated. Interestingly, Wilczynski suggested that the difference in gender motives might reflect exaggerations of social roles.

In terms of her classification system, Wilczynski cautioned: "It should be stressed however, that further research needs to be carried out to determine whether the classification proposed here should be modified or refined further when different—and larger—samples of filicide are considered."[33]

It is clear that there have been numerous attempts to articulate a comprehensive classification system related to mothers who kill their children. The last classification system to be discussed here,[34] and the only one which was based exclusively on a sample of U.S. women, was presented by Oberman in 1996. Oberman's classification system was based on some unique premises. As she indicated,

> Many women who commit infanticide do so while suffering from an identifiable mental disability that renders them temporarily or permanently incapable of caring for themselves and/or their children without considerable outside assistance. It is critical to note at the outset that it is not the fact of mental illness or disability alone, but rather the combination of a vulnerable mental health status and social isolation that leads to infanticide. My analysis begins by addressing issues of mental health status, and then explores the intersection of social isolation, mothering, and mental health.[35]

In Oberman's typology the interaction of mental illness and social factors is explored within each category of the classification system.

Oberman classified cases into two categories which included neonaticide and infanticide. Infanticide was further subdivided into infanticide and postpartum psychosis, infanticide by mothers with chronic mental disabilities, infanticide as a manifestation of an affective disorder with postpartum onset, and addiction-related infanticide. Oberman's typology evolved from a review of cases that she obtained through NEXIS searching. NEXIS is a news database which provides full text articles and publications from newsmagazines, regional and national newspapers, newsletters, trade magazines, and abstracts. Transcripts of various news-related media, such as radio and television news broadcasts, are also accessible. Using detailed search strategies, Oberman assessed the news accounts of more than ninety-six cases, namely, forty-nine filicide cases and forty-seven neonaticide cases. Oberman did not address exactly how many of the forty-nine cases fell into each infanticide category but she describes each category extensively with illustrative case studies. Moreover she includes extensive tables and charts addressing the characteristics of neonaticidal and infanticidal mothers.

Our Research

Oberman's cases provided the impetus for the present typology. We believed that the unique interaction of social, environmental, cultural, and individual variables needed to be addressed *within each category* of filicidal mothers, so that we could arrive at as complete a picture as possible of the factors which come together to result in filicide in each case. It was also clear to us that a typology relevant to the U.S. cases needed to be developed. We began our endeavor by reading all of Oberman's cases. From this reading each member of the research team, working independently, created a typology. Then our research group combined our classifications into a single working draft of a typology that underwent many revisions. As we reviewed previous cases and classifications systems, our data and analysis supported some prior categories while others received little or no support. What is truly unique about our typology is that we have created a detailed characterization within each category of that particular type of filicidal mother instead of just noting overall risk factors. Therefore we were able to outline specific social and policy implications and intervention strategies.

The primary researchers for this project were Michelle Oberman and Cheryl Meyer. However, it was quickly apparent that for the research project to be completed in a timely manner, a team of researchers would be required to help gather information and conceptualize the cases. The team included Priya Batra, Tara Proano, Michelle Rone, and Kelly White. The research team represented a diverse professional group including a lawyer with a MPH, a social psychologist with a law degree, two clinical psychologists, and two clinical psychologists in training. It was clear that the topic required the expertise of legal scholars as well as psychologists to be comprehensive and accurate. All the researchers were familiar with searching NEXIS. However, as Oberman discovered, searching for infanticide cases required some creativity. Although the scholarly literature may refer to the killing of a child as neonaticide, filicide, or infanticide, the terminology used by the popular media is much more colloquial. It became necessary to devise elaborate search strings to access the cases relevant to our topic. For example, searching the terms "mother," and "child," and "kill" (and their variants) would have yielded thousands of cases, including many in which mother and child were killed in a car accident or the child killed the mother.

We selected January 1990 to December 1999 as a target period and searched each year, using two different sets of search terms.[36] Three independent reviewers from the research team read every relevant case. For the most part they were able to agree as to the case's fit within a certain category. Such cases were given to the researcher who was primarily responsible for that category and chapter. Cases that did not clearly fit a category were discussed and tentatively assigned to a particular category until more information could be found on them.

When the cases had been separated into categories, the researcher for that category followed up each one in regional databases. For example, if a neonaticide case had occurred in Chicago, the researcher for that case would assess the NEXIS regional databases and local news resources (e.g., the *Chicago Tribune*) for the years following the initial report in order to determine the disposition of the case and access further details. Cases which could not be followed up extensively through further searching were deleted from the sample. These included cases in which the mother was never located or the name of the mother was not released because she was a juvenile. Additionally, if more extensive searching revealed that a case had been assigned to the wrong category, it was transferred to the right one. Finally, some new cases appeared during regional searches but were not included in the analysis in order to keep search strategies as standardized as possible.

We excluded international cases from the analysis since our focus was on the United States. Cases in which a mother killed an adopted child (which were rare) were not used to create the typology because they often involved unique dynamics.[37] In addition, cases where the mother attempted murder but the child survived were excluded from analysis. Cases where someone else killed the child (e.g., the father or a boyfriend) and the mother was not charged with murder were also eliminated. Finally, Munchausen by Proxy cases were not included since one of the mother's main goals in such cases was to bring attention to herself, and the death of the child not only was unintended but also defeated this goal. Only cases that occurred during the target period, including those assessed by our searches and through Michelle Oberman's original searches, were used to formulate the typology. However, a few well-known or historical cases, although outside the scope of our time period, were included in this book.

We tracked some characteristics and circumstances across all the cases. These included age of mother, age and gender of child, method of death, marital status, number of children in the family and in the home, geographical location, date of crime, charge/conviction, mother's behavioral response after death, history of domestic violence, mental health and substance abuse history, socioeconomic status, the need for public assistance, children's protective service involvement, frequency of weapon use, any motive mentioned, and birth order of child. The researchers recorded the available information related to these characteristics for each case within their category in order to determine patterns. In addition, the researcher for each category also tracked characteristics which were specific to the category.

Advantages and Disadvantages of Using NEXIS as a Data Source

Prior to collecting any cases, we conducted a comprehensive search of all the scholarly literature available on infanticide, filicide, or neonaticide. In all, we searched twenty-three databases, including MEDLINE, PsycInfo, Bioethicsline, LEXIS, Social Sciences Index, and Dissertation Abstracts.[38] The searches did not yield very many citations, particularly when the literature regarding international trends was eliminated. There were less than fifty books or articles directly related to our topic. Most of these citations were theoretical pieces with little or no empirical basis. Although filicide is apparently a very frequent phenomenon, there has been scant empirical investigation of it. As Wilczynski notes, "The first major limitation of the research on child homicide is simply its paucity."[39]

This is probably due to the fact that it is difficult, and in some cases impossible (as with juveniles), to access information about the crimes and perpetrators. One way to access data would be to look at convictions for homicide. However, cases tried in juvenile court would still have been lost using such a method, as would cases in which the women who were arrested for murder pled guilty to a lesser offense. Women who committed murder-suicide would also be lost in this type of analysis. Finally, using such a method would necessitate perusing the arrests and conviction records of several major cities to provide a large enough sample size to create a typology. In fact, a quick examination of prior empirical research demonstrates the difficulties inherent in such techniques.[40] Using NEXIS as a data source provided greater access to cases and therefore increased the number of cases available for review.

However, as with any design and methodology, the advantages are offset by disadvantages. Perhaps the greatest drawback to using this approach was the fact that articles or transcripts were subject to the biases and accuracy of the reporter. We therefore approached the data with much skepticism. However, most of the cases, especially the ones we chose to highlight, were followed up extensively by numerous reporters and in various resources. This provided us an opportunity to verify many details of each case.[41] In addition, the volume of cases we were able to assess compensated somewhat for the inaccuracies of this methodology, especially given that the small number of accessible cases has been noted as a flaw in previous classification attempts.

Other frequently used methods are also susceptible to such biases. For example, public records are often used as a data source. Qualitative public records, such as police reports, are subject to the individual biases of the officer, yet these data sources are nonetheless considered legitimate. Wilczynski has observed that

> as with much of the research on child maltreatment, it [the literature] draws on selective and unrepresentative samples. Most studies include suspects identified at particular stages of the criminal justice system, typically those institutionalised in a prison or forensic psychiatric service. Other studies draw on samples which are also systematically biased—for example, cases referred previously or subsequently to child protection services. Often suspects who commit suicide are excluded. Few studies

have gathered data on cases identified at earlier stages of the criminal justice system (for example, using coroners', police or hospital records), where the filtering and processing of this system have much less impact.[42]

Finally, the utility of NEXIS and/or newspapers as a data source has previously been demonstrated by other researchers who have used it to create profiles of juvenile offenders[43] and to supplement other methods of data collection on infanticide.[44] Moreover, the need for a current U.S. typology outweighed even our most serious methodological concerns, especially given the problems with previous systems.

The Typology

We offer five categories or types in our typology. Each type will be discussed extensively in a separate chapter. However, a summary of the types and the rationale behind their development is presented here. Some types naturally broke down into subtypes while others did not.

A distinctive feature of our typology is that, unlike other classification systems, it is not based on motive or intent but describes the patterns associated with filicides from an interactional perspective, encompassing a wide array of social, cultural, environmental, and individual variables.

Filicide Related to an Ignored Pregnancy

The women in this category either denied or concealed their pregnancies. All of them committed neonaticide. Most of them were juveniles. Previous typologies have included a category similar to this one but have suggested that the mother always denied the pregnancy.[45] We thought such a characterization was limited since we found that while some women who committed neonaticide denied their condition, others actively concealed their pregnancy but never actually denied it. Instead, they were unable to discuss it with anyone or discussed it with only a select few.

Abuse-Related Filicide

This category includes mothers who killed their child during a physical assault. Although these women had previously assaulted their child or children, the purpose of the assault was not to kill the child. Often the alleged purpose of the abuse was discipline.

Filicide Due to Neglect

These mothers did not purposely kill their child but either failed to attend to the child's basic needs or were irresponsible in their reaction to the child's behavior. Therefore, these cases subdivide into *neglect-omission* and *neglect-commission,* respectively. Neglect-omission includes instances in which the mother did not attend to the health, nutrition, or safety needs of the child, such as leaving children in a closed car in hot weather. Neglect-commission includes cases in which an irresponsible action by the mother caused the death, such as shaking the baby too hard or placing something over the child's head to stop the child from crying.

Assisted/Coerced Filicide

We included a case in this category if the mother killed the child, or if her partner—generally a romantic partner—did the killing and the mother was charged with murder. It was not unusual to find cases in which the partner killed the child and the mother was charged with a lesser crime such as child endangerment. But such cases were not included in our analysis.

Purposeful Filicide and the Mother Acted Alone

This type was the most challenging of the entire typology. Originally we divided it into two types, purposeful filicide with and without mental illness. Initially, we thought that mental illness distinguished these women. For example, the women who were suffering from postpartum psychosis and killed their children because they perceived the child as the devil were clearly suffering from a mental illness. Similarly, the women who killed their children and then committed suicide seemed to be suffering from a mental illness. However, most of these women had not been officially diagnosed, either because a diagnosis did not exist[46] or because the woman did not have or did not seek assistance from a healthcare provider. This raised concerns about what constituted mental illness and whether a formal diagnosis was necessary to assert that the woman had a mental illness. These concerns were magnified when we considered the cases we had previously determined to have been "without" mental illness. Our struggles with definitions of mental illness became the basis for this chapter.

Our data set included 219 cases. The majority were neglect cases (76), purposeful cases (79), and neonaticide cases (37). Interestingly, filicides due to abuse represented the smallest number of cases, with 15 in the maternal abuse category and 12 in the assisted/coerced category.

In the following five chapters (chapters 2 through 6) we discuss each of our categories in depth. We include our characterization of the mothers who were in that category, empirical research related to the patterns the mothers exhibited, and a discussion of social and policy implications. Finally, we outline potential interventions. In the final chapter (chapter 7) we discuss the implications of our findings.

2

DENIAL OF PREGNANCY

Secret Lives

❏

There are neonaticide cases that we all somehow know, those that have touched the collective consciousness—for example, the girl who gave birth at her senior prom in the suburbs of New Jersey and the college-aged couple who brought a child into the world within the confines of a Comfort Inn in Delaware; both these babies would later die at the hands of their mothers. Beyond the cases that earn rabid media coverage, a nationwide phenomenon is occurring. Babies killed within a few hours of their births are not rare events and yet we continue to react with horror whenever a new case is brought to light. We seem unable to answer many fundamental questions. This chapter aims to dispel some of the shock value of such cases by demonstrating the remarkably patterned nature of neonaticide in contemporary U.S. society. Consider the following case:

Marianne Biancuzzo, age nineteen, of Arizona lived with her parents and fif-teen-year-old brother in what was described as an "outwardly whole and happy family."[1] *In November 1997 she gave birth to a baby girl in one of the bathrooms of her family's home. At the time she began going into labor, Marianne claimed she believed herself to be only four to five months pregnant. On the day she gave birth, she initially assumed that she was physically ill and only later realized she was in labor. It was reported in newspaper accounts that she gave birth over the toilet. The official cause of death was determined to be drowning.*

Afterwards, the child's remains were placed in a coffee can and stored beneath the sink. Marianne later gave statements alleging it was her intention to bury the remains in the backyard but the plan was thwarted when her brother accidentally discovered the contents in the coffee can. Family and friends all claimed not to have known she was pregnant. Marianne asserted that the reason she did not reach out for help after realizing she was pregnant was because she did not want her family to know of her condition. Marianne was eventually charged with first-degree murder and child abuse. Before the case went to trial, she was released on $25,000 bail and kept under house arrest. She was eventually found guilty of negligent homicide (the lowest charge considered by the jury), sentenced to one year in prison, a $1,200 fine, and three years of probation.

Many features of Marianne's situation are consistent with other contemporary U.S. neonaticide cases included in our study. Her age, her marital status, the apparent absence of her baby's father, her failure to acknowledge and disclose her pregnancy to others, and the fact that she endured labor alone are all factors common to the overwhelming majority of the cases in this study. This chapter will further develop the patterns common to the phenomenon of neonaticide. It begins by briefly reviewing the scholarship on this enigmatic behavior. Following this review we discuss the neonaticide data generated by our study. This discussion reveals the dramatic patterns underlying such cases, and helps to create a more nuanced understanding of the phenomenon. Building upon this foundation, the chapter then moves to an assessment of the underlying causes of neonaticide. The final section of the chapter includes a discussion of the contemporary policies surrounding neonaticide, including the erratic responses of the criminal justice system to those who commit neonaticide. The chapter closes with policy suggestions aimed at minimizing, if not preventing, the occurrence of this tragic crime.

Neonaticide Research

Several generations of scholars have studied the phenomenon of infanticide. Their findings suggest that homicide rates for children under one year of age are as high, and possibly even higher, than adult rates. Homicide rates for infants have remained consistent over the past several decades while overall murder rates have steadily increased. Children aged one through four have significantly lower rates of traumatic death than do younger children.[2] In 1969, Phillip Resnick first coined the term neonaticide to refer to death by homicide within the first twenty-four hours of life.[3] Neonaticide is a remarkably widespread phenomenon. Indeed, one study estimates that 45 percent of children murdered before age one die within twenty-four hours of the onset of their lives, thus making them victims of neonaticide.[4] Despite the patterns underlying such homicides, there is considerable uncertainty about the source of this behavior.

To date, Resnick remains the most frequently cited scholar on the broad category of filicide and specifically on the phenomenon of neonaticide. His research posits that the vast majority of neonaticides occur because the women involved simply do not want their children. His initial understanding of this phenomenon was limited, however, by the weaknesses of his research methodology. His conclusions were predicated not upon actual work with the subject population, but on his having read thirty-seven case reports of neonaticide, translated from thirteen different languages, that occurred between 1751 and 1967. Despite such shortcomings, researchers continue to compare their findings to his when further examinations of neonaticide are conducted.

In the decades since Resnick's article, many other authors have undertaken to describe and explain the dynamics of neonaticide. Theories as to why this behavior has occurred throughout time have ranged vastly. Some contend that the causes for neonaticide reflect biological or evolutionary imperatives, in other words, that there is a capacity for neonaticide is built into human genetic design.[5] Others shun such explanations in favor of more psychologically and sociologically bound theories. Some, for instance, have attempted to blame neonaticide on a "culture of violence." Upon closer examination, this explanation is untenable.[6] Using data from the World Health Organization, Lester determined that the rates at which newborns are killed do not correlate with overall societal murder rates, but do show a relation to suicide rates. In other words, as suicide rates increase, so do national neonaticide rates. Lester concludes that this means that neonaticide is more closely associated with self-destructive rather than with homicidal impulses.[7]

Many contemporary scholars focus upon the psychological and environmental factors influencing the perpetrators of neonaticide. Bourget and Labelle reasserted many of Resnick's positions when they stated the following: "Most neonaticides are the results of unwanted pregnancies and births. Mothers tend to be younger and unwed, and the inability of the girl to reveal her pregnancy to her mother, the stigma of having an illegitimate child, and the shame or fear of rejection are factors in many cases."[8] They proceeded to note that many of the women who commit neonaticide have personality characteristics marked by immaturity, impulsivity, or antisocial traits. Resnick cited work from 1938 when he claimed that the predominant personality trait in neonaticidal women was passivity.[9]

Researchers have identified numerous demographic consistencies among neonaticidal women. In their review of the infanticide literature, Cummings, Theis, Mueller, and Rivara[10] found that risk factors associated with infant death in general are young maternal age, maternal lack of education, low birth weight of child, unmarried mother, and late or no prenatal care. This information is interesting in light of specific data related to the phenomenon of neonaticide. Emerick, Foster, and Campbell studied 146 traumatic infant deaths in Oregon between 1973 and 1982, focusing on risk factors for filicidal behavior.[11] Eight of the cases examined were classified as neonaticides. Factors found to be the most associated with neonaticide were unwed motherhood, late or no prenatal care, and non-hospital births. Another study found that 95 percent of infants killed during the first day of life were not born in a hospital, compared to the fact that only 8 percent of all children killed during their first year of life were born in non-hospital locations.[12] Other researchers have supported these findings and have also indicated that first-time motherhood[13] and social and economic stresses[14] are additional common features of neonaticide.

These factors are perhaps best understood in the context of what we know about the women who commit neonaticide and the events that lead to the infant's demise. Research suggests that neonaticide is not a premeditated act, but rather an act committed in the face of intense emotion such as shock, shame, guilt, and fear.[15] As Alder and Baker have noted, "[I]t would be inappropriate and unenlightening to depict these events as moments of anger or rage, or eruptions of extreme uncontrolled aggression. These scenarios do reveal the burden of responsibility for contraception that is borne by women in our society, and the continuing negative consequences for young women of single parenthood."[16] Severe mental illness is unusual among those who commit neonaticide.[17] Instead, their problems appear to lie in the realm of relationships, access to resources, and sense of self.

More often than not, the woman who commits neonaticide is in her teenage years and overwhelmed by the possibility of being pregnant, let alone dealing with the prospect of choosing a course for resolving the pregnancy. For a myriad of reasons, she hides her pregnancy from family and friends. Brezinka, Huter, Biebl, and Kinzl[18] state that the presence of psychosocial stressors are often predisposing factors toward later denial of pregnancy. Examples of such stressors include separation from a partner, financial hardship, physical and/or mental illness, and interpersonal problems. These psychosocial stressors may have an influence upon the young woman's physical symptoms and experiences of pregnancy. For example, Brezinka's research team studied twenty-seven women in Austria between 1987 and 1990 who denied their pregnancies. Of these, only seven were amenorrheic, twelve had irregular spotting, two had continuous spotting, four had regular menstrual periods, and two were unable to report their menstrual histories. Fifteen of the twenty-seven gained little or no weight. None of the women had typical nausea symptoms. These numbers exemplify the fact that physiological aberrations can occur as a result of complex psychological mechanisms.

Shame and guilt have frequently been cited as precursors to concealment of pregnancy. The sources of such feelings have been linked to many possibilities. These include ambivalence about sexuality (e.g., having enjoyed sex versus mixed feelings about having engaged in intercourse before truly ready), and embarrassment pertaining to misuse of, misinformation about, or ignorance surrounding contraception. Many girls and women may feel ashamed about having engaged in sexual relations, and fearful that their pregnancies will disappoint and even humiliate their families.[19] Although some girls may purposely choose to conceal their pregnancies, others are in such deep denial that they never make a conscious decision regarding concealment. Indeed, some scholars of neonaticide note that "the line between conscious and unconscious denial is not a fixed one."[20]

The guiding emotion for some who commit neonaticide may be fear rather than shame or guilt. Women may fear the reactions of an underinvolved or abusive sexual partner. Some may worry about parents' reactions to pregnancy status, fearing that they will literally become homeless and emotionally cut off from their families. As a result, some young women become terrified by the harsh realization that they cannot financially handle the responsibility of existing as a single parent. Economic marginalization has been cited as a strong contributing factor to later neonaticidal behavior.[21]

The way neonaticide is committed shows consistent patterns. Increasingly violent means of death occur as the children get older. However, Smithey[22] has noted that the risk of fatal injury actually decreases with each additional day of life. As less force is required to kill a neonate than an infant or other young child, it is not surprising that less violent means are used.

Neonaticides tend to be relatively nonviolent deaths. Means of death are typically strangulation and suffocation, followed by head trauma, drowning, exposure, and stabbing.[23] These rates clearly differentiate neonaticide cases from other filicide cases, in which the predominant causes of death are battering and assault.[24] The use of weapons is far more likely in an infanticide[25] than a neonaticide.[26]

A psychological theory pertaining to the dynamics of filicide has been offered by Crimmins, Langley, Brownstein, and Spunt.[27] They note, "[T]he woman's sense of self is too damaged for her to care about another human being. Self becomes damaged not simply because trauma occurs but also because an absence of social supports and an inability to rely upon others in times of need lays the foundation for the message that self is unimportant."[28] They conducted extensive interviews with forty-two women who were convicted of killing their children (of all different ages). In sharing their advice about how to prevent other women from making the same mistakes that they did, 45 percent of the interviewees stated that programs for enhancing self-esteem are greatly needed. A strong sense of connection with others, in addition to the belief that one can make life-impacting decisions appropriately, are factors could help alter national rates of neonaticide.

One recent study suggests that currently available frameworks fail to take important cultural factors into consideration and thereby provide an incomplete understanding of infanticide in general, and of neonaticide in particular. Silva and his colleagues assert that an understanding of neonaticidal women's motivations and behaviors can only be understood from a "biopsychosociocultural" perspective.[29] Only when contextual factors (specifically the biological, psychological, sociological, and cultural) are considered may we begin to understand the persistence of neonaticide in contemporary society. In the following sections, this chapter undertakes to explore neonaticide from this richly nuanced perspective.

The Current Research

Why is this happening and what can be done to curb the number of girls and women who commit neonaticide each year? Although researchers have attempted to answer these questions over the years, the body of literature remains inconclusive and lacking in definitive suggestions as to appropriate and effective means for handling the problem. Ultimately, our research yielded 37 cases deemed sufficiently complete and suitable for inclusion in this chapter, although the estimates for annual occurrence of neonaticide range between 150 and 300.[30]

Although there are many possible reasons why we were unable to amass more cases, three reasons stand out as the most prominent. First and foremost, the act of neonaticide often goes undetected. Though hard to comprehend at first, women over time have found various means to conceal their pregnancies. When no one with whom they regularly interact is awaiting the birth of a child, it becomes that much easier to surreptitiously hide or bury a deceased baby subsequent to childbirth. Indeed, the identities of the mothers of many newborn corpses are never determined.[31] Second, media outlets consciously choose the types of stories they believe will bolster their sales and ratings. It is possible that as a nation we have collectively become callous in the face of certain acts among particular populations of people. In other words, the media may have tacitly determined that many of these stories are simply so mundane that they are not "newsworthy." Finally, many neonaticides go unreported by the mass media due to the mother's young age and related injunctions against releasing her identity.

Therefore, we report our findings with the caveat that this chapter reflects trends that were apparent among thirty-seven well-reported cases of neonaticide that occurred in the United States between 1990 and 1999. While this number is by no means an exhaustive representation of all the incidents that have truly occurred, it is a representative subsample. We included herein a discussion of women from varying races, ethnic backgrounds, socioeconomic standings, religions, and walks of life who committed neonaticide. It is our hope and intention that their stories will permit a more empathic and comprehensive understanding of why a woman would resort to so desperate an act.

Contemporary Depictions of Neonaticide: A Survey of Cases from 1990 to 1999

The facts about neonaticide are more complex than those details to which we are typically exposed on television. It is quite possible that the media selects girls like Rebecca Hopfer, Audrey Iacona, Amy Grossberg, and Melissa Drexler because they are the least likely to come to mind when we think of mothers killing their newborns. Because they were relatively affluent, attractive young white girls from seemingly "good" families, their crimes are shocking and therefore deemed newsworthy. This implies that neonaticide is somehow understandable, if not excusable, when committed by poorer, more desperate women, or for that matter, a woman of color. When we observe the consistent patterns that underlie such cases, the crime of neonaticide appears far less enigmatic than one might imagine it to be.

Although the cases in our study include other neonaticides committed by young white girls from relatively affluent families, they are far from prototypical. In fact, the ages of women in our sample ranged from fifteen to thirty-nine, and the average age among our thirty-seven cases was 19.3. Additionally—although this is somewhat difficult to definitively ascertain from newspaper accounts—it is clear that ethnic minorities committed a significant number of these crimes, and that they came from diverse socioeconomic backgrounds. Though Rebecca, Audrey, Amy, and Melissa did not have any other children, fourteen of the thirty-seven women we studied had other children before committing neonaticide. Their children's ages ranged from less than one year to eleven. Only two were reported as having received abortions in the past.[32] Additionally, and perhaps most troubling, four of these women had previously committed, or attempted to commit, another neonaticide. Regarding the pregnancies that subsequently led to neonaticides, it is difficult to discern how many women were under medical attention or had at least one prenatal examination by a physician. However, the number is likely to be close to zero given scant media accounts. In only one case was there mention of a neonaticidal woman having received medical care for her pregnancy prior to going into labor.[33]

Thirty-six of the thirty-seven women in our sample were single—only one was reportedly married. This most consistent of factors linking all the cases is, ironically, almost entirely ignored by both the media and the criminal justice system. Indeed, one of the most striking aspects of the media coverage is the lack of focus on and discussion about the males who impregnated the women concerned. Even in court, many judges ruled that the identity of the deceased child's father was inconsequential to the proceedings. When the women's relationships to the men were discussed in newspaper accounts, the women most often reported that they were no longer involved in intimate relationships with the men by whom they became pregnant. Several of the intimate relationships were reported to have lasted only a short period of time or to have ended when a future father found out about the pregnancy. Oberman's[34] study of forty-seven neonaticide cases noted a trend toward "highly unstable liaisons" between the women and their lovers. Women who commit neonaticide are rarely part of harmonious, stable, and loving relational partnerships.

Amy Grossberg was reportedly the only woman of the thirty-seven who had someone else present while undergoing childbirth. According to newspaper accounts, fourteen of the women gave birth in their bathrooms at home, three in a bedroom, and twelve in an undisclosed location within their homes. Other locations reported included a campsite, public bathroom, motel, family garage, a portable toilet in an onion field, and an alleyway. Locations for labor were not reported for the remaining two cases. While an argument could be made that these women purposefully chose surreptitious locations in which to undergo labor, one could also surmise that they unexpectedly started experiencing labor in inopportune places. Close study of the cases reveals that even those women who had acknowledged that they were pregnant were surprised by and completely unprepared for the onset of labor.

At this point, it is critical to revisit the factors that contribute to the act of neonaticide. Though media accounts may err on the side of sensationalizing the stories or suggesting hypotheses mired in hype rather than fact, trends emerge when the women's voices are allowed to come forth. As noted in the literature review, psychosocial stressors are often strong contributing factors presaging such behavior. Recall that the literature on neonaticide reports that the young women tend to be overwhelmed by feelings of shame, guilt, and fear. In our sample, these emotions were fairly readily identified, even through the ordinarily dry medium of newspaper articles.

First of all, there were numerous instances in which the girls feared that by disclosing their pregnancies they might jeopardize their relationships with families and partners. Some girls reported fearing that they would be asked to leave their homes by parents who strongly disapproved of premarital sex. Others had explicitly been told in the past that if they were to get pregnant again they would no longer be permitted to stay with their families. Still others reported their fear of losing a boyfriend should he come to know of the pregnancy.

In addition to fearing the loss of family and/or relationship, many of the women in our sample labored under other sources of stress as well. For example, several of them were new immigrants to the United States. In other instances, the pregnant woman was undocumented and the pregnancy threatened to expose her illegal residence in the United States. For yet other women, the pregnancy triggered conflicts that grew out of the religious and social values governing sexuality that inhered in their cultures of origin. Finally, being new immigrants, the women faced financial hardships, and the unwanted pregnancies surely contributed to a sense of economic precariousness.

Of the thirty-seven cases examined in this chapter, the methods of killing were also fairly consistent with those mentioned in the literature. As expected, most committed neonaticide through strangulation or suffocation. Twenty-six of the newborns ultimately died from being smothered after being put in the trash, a dumpster, or elsewhere (e.g., buried in a yard or left in a closet under a pile of clothes). Some of the babies were put in these locations while still alive, while others had already been asphyxiated beforehand. Four women left their babies outside, causing them to die of exposure. Five newborns were drowned in either a bathtub or toilet and three were killed by more violent means (e.g., baseball clubbing, stabbing, and being thrown to pitbull dogs). In only one case, that of Summer McKee, was a history of mental illness reported by the media.

Specific Accounts of Neonaticide

One need not read scores of neonaticide cases in order to observe their patterned nature. Indeed, in spite of their superficial differences in terms of geography, ethnicity, and age the commonalities linking the women who commit neonaticide are readily apparent. Consider the following cases:

Rachel Anglum was eighteen years old when she gave birth to a baby girl at the home where she lived with her parents. She allegedly delivered the baby alone and afterwards held her daughter in her arms for over an hour. It was later determined that "she hugged her newborn to death"[35] *and subsequently wrapped the* *baby's remains in a blanket, put her in a heavy-duty garbage bag, and drove to a dumpster a few miles from her home. The body was later discovered by two men looking through the dumpster for boxes. Rachel was eventually indicted on a charge of second-degree murder and released on $9,420 bail. There were no reports of how this case ended.*

Linda Chu was a twenty-year-old student at the University of Southern California when she went into labor in her dormitory suite. A strangled infant's corpse was later found in the trash chute. Linda is an Asian-American. When students were asked by the police if they knew of any pregnant Asian-American women on campus, they were unable to make a positive identification. Six weeks later, investigators identified her as the mother of the deceased child. Subsequently she was extradited back to California from Illinois where she had been staying with her family for summer break. Friends and family later stated that none of them knew she had ever been pregnant. After being indicted on a number of different charges, Linda finally pled no contest to felony child abuse and was sentenced to ten years in prison with a stipulation that a minimum of five years be served.

Julie Quinn, age thirty, gave birth in the bathtub of the apartment where she lived with her boyfriend. Four days after her child was born she told her boyfriend that not only had she been pregnant, but that she had given birth alone and then put the baby in the closet under a pile of blankets and clothes. At this point in time, the child was already dead. Julie was ultimately convicted of first degree reckless homicide and sentenced to twenty-five years in prison with eligibility for parole after six years.

Given their young age, unmarried status, and concealment of pregnancy from all those around them, Rachel and Linda clearly fit the standard profile of neonaticidal women. Although she was somewhat older and resided with her boyfriend, Julie nonetheless illustrated some of the typical features of this profile as well. She never told her boyfriend that she was pregnant. Like the other two women, Julie was unwed, had no prenatal care, and gave birth in a nonmedical environment. None of the three women had any other children.

The themes previously mentioned as common to neonaticides are made vivid by these three examples. Each of the women was remarkably isolated in spite of the fact that there were many others around them in a position to observe their status. Thus, they became paralyzed and unable to craft a meaningful response to their pregnancies. Though Rachel was initially described as a popular and well-adjusted girl, later accounts stated that she became terrified by the prospect of her parents finding out she had become pregnant. The father of her baby was a young man she had been dating for a year. No other information is known about him except that he was unaware of Rachel's pregnancy and uninvolved in the neonaticide. Press coverage of Linda described her as a shy young woman who chose not to live in the dorms because she would be forced to interact with too many people. Although reportedly from a privileged background, it is unknown what type of relationship she had with her parents and what access to private funds she herself had. The identity of the father of Linda's baby is unknown.

Julie was living with her boyfriend, and therefore may at first blush seem to present a different situation from that of Rachel and Linda. It is clear that she did not confide in her partner about her condition. She later stated that she kept her condition a secret because she thought her boyfriend would leave her, as he had previously indicated he was disinterested in having children. Indeed, her boyfriend terminated their relationship upon her arrest. What does distinguish Julie's case from that of the others is that during her trial it was alleged that she had previously committed another neonaticide at the age of twenty. However, little is known about the circumstances under which the alleged neonaticide occurred.[36] Insofar as the current case is concerned, we know that although she lived with her boyfriend, she was so isolated from him and from others that she felt unable to seek assistance in resolving the problem posed by her pregnancy.

In spite of age, race, and class differences, these three women are fairly typical representatives of neonaticide. Overwhelmed by fear and shame due to an unplanned pregnancy, all concealed their conditions for months and later went through labor alone in their homes. All were unmarried and had no other children; none had a reported history of mental health problems. Each of their babies died either through strangulation or suffocation.

Underlying Causes of Contemporary Neonaticide

Denial

Many leading neonaticide researchers have spoken about the "massive denial" manifested by women who commit this crime.[37] They attribute this denial to the tremendous fear surrounding the repercussions of the pregnancy. Although some would assert that active fear and pervasive denial are mutually exclusive cognitive states, it can also be argued that those women who ultimately commit neonaticide may in fact contend with both types of thought processes at different points during their pregnancies. Some of these girls and women may have been conscious of their pregnancies, but unable to make decisions about how to proceed. Instead, they may simply have put off deciding, day after day, throughout the long months of their pregnancies.

Others may have been so dominated by confusion and fear that they simply moved into a complete denial of their pregnancies. For at least some of these women, the denial ran so deep that they physically continued to menstruate and gained only a minimal amount of weight. This is a well-documented phenomenon, as noted previously.[38] Indeed, many reports state that upon giving birth the women were surprised to find that what they thought were abdominal cramps, indigestion, or a need to defecate were actually indicators of imminent childbirth. Margaret Spinelli, a forensic psychiatrist, has worked with several neonaticidal women who later described having experienced a dissociative episode during childbirth. Many of them were horrified to later discover what had become of their infants.[39]

One of the important consequences of denial in the foregoing cases is that the pregnant woman will not form a significant affective bond with the fetus. Women who are conflicted, ambivalent, and/or horrified about their pregnancies are likely to experience little of the bonding to the fetus that women experience during wanted pregnancies. In light of this, it may be easier to understand the neonaticidal woman's ability to put the baby out of her mind once she has given birth to it. In a sense, her act is one of confusion and panic, not one of anger. It is this aspect of such cases—the complete absence of any healthy psychological and physical bonds between the mother and the child—which distinguishes the act of neonaticide from all the other types of filicide.

Remorse

As discussed previously, many of the young women who commit neonaticide are immature and lack resources, both economical and psychological, to effectively solve problems. Given the psychology of adolescence, it is not surprising that many of them put off making a decision about their pregnancies or fail to contemplate the possible long-term repercussions of not acting upon their unwanted pregnancies. Denial, therefore, can be understood to be fairly age-appropriate behavior.

The inability to cope early on with the fact that one is pregnant directly impacts the ability to secure an abortion. Though laws vary by state, the most affordable and available abortion services are offered during the first trimester (i.e., twelve weeks' gestation). Furthermore, many of the girls come from religious and familial backgrounds wherein abortion is unsupported and condemned as murder. Oberman argues that these factors can lead to an inner conflict and profound sense of ambivalence among many girls, causing them to procrastinate rather than making a difficult decision.[40] As the pregnancy progresses, they continue to put off the decision about what to do and come to ignore the fact that no decision has been made. When the baby ultimately arrives, they are actually taken by surprise.

Mental Status

Just because a young woman is in denial about her pregnancy does not automatically imply the presence of profound psychosis or some other mental illness. Instead, the denial is often a temporary state that may vary in depth among individuals. For example, it is very common for women who have committed neonaticide to report no memory of having given birth. Many report a more profound denial, though, and are unable to recall having been pregnant in the first place. Brezinka, Huter, Biebl, and Kinzl specifically studied the topic of women who denied pregnancy and determined that "(d)enial of pregnancy is a heterogeneous condition with different meanings and different psychiatric diagnoses in different women."[41] Plainly, the experience of denial in neonaticidal women serves to illustrate the aforementioned point that there are not clear distinctive boundaries between conscious and unconscious denial.[42]

Nonetheless, it is clear that some small percentage of women who commit neonaticide do suffer from mental illnesses before and/or during their pregnancies. Studies estimate that just under 30 percent of neonaticidal women suffered from preexisting mental illnesses.[43] This stands in contrast to McKee and Shea's[44] finding that approximately 80 percent of filicidal parents had psychiatric symptoms prior to their criminal act and 15 percent had been psychiatrically hospitalized prior to killing their children.[45] It is difficult to discern evidence of such mental illness from media accounts. However, one of the cases in our study describes a young woman with a detailed history of psychological problems prior to her committing neonaticide. Summer McKee was twenty years old when she gave birth alone, in her parents' home. The body of her daughter was later found asphyxiated in the trunk of her car. The media stories about her case noted that she had long suffered from major depressive disorder, and had been hospitalized for this condition in the past. Given the media's tendency to sensationalize stories with a mental health component, it is all the more likely that evidence of such conditions, if it existed, would have gotten mention in the media stories pertinent to this chapter.

Questionable Support Systems

Many of these stories describe young women who gained weight and whose bodies underwent physical changes. And yet their appearances went unnoticed, or simply unmentioned, by those who were closest to them. Almost all the women were living with family members during their pregnancies, labors, and deliveries. It is remarkable that none of the adults in these women's lives noticed the physical and psychological changes of pregnancy that they were undergoing. The media tends to excuse this inattentiveness on the grounds that the young women "concealed" their pregnancies. If one thinks about this critically, however, it is obvious that it is quite difficult to conceal a pregnancy for months from those with whom one is sharing a bathroom or a dorm room or even a hallway.

Instead, it seems likely that this lack of communication tells us something about the quality of their relationships. Most importantly, it appears that the relationships were not sufficiently intimate to permit the pregnant girl or woman to confide in them. Nor were they sufficiently close, open, or safe enough for family members or friends to have approached the pregnant female. When asked about their failure to reveal their pregnancies to their families, many of the girls reported their fear that they would be exiled from their loved ones. Several had previously been pregnant, and were explicitly told by family members that they would be asked to move out or denied any support should they become pregnant once again. Other girls reported being fearful about their families finding out about the race of their sexual partner. Still others explained that they did not want to disappoint their families by having

56

become pregnant and thus did not disclose their condition for this reason. These fears reveal common themes about the extent to which an unwanted pregnancy might be perceived as a threat to one's entire social system, and might lead both a young woman and those around her to collaborate in the denial of a pregnancy.

These points highlight how even an apparently advantaged woman can be paralyzed by a perceived lack of resources. Unappealing options (e.g., choosing between undergoing an abortion or telling an unsupportive or disapproving family of the pregnancy) and limited access to necessary resources (e.g., anonymity, money, transportation, unconditional support, and the like) leave the girl with no viable recourse. Morris and Wilczynski studied 474 cases of filicide that occurred in England between 1982 and 1989. After much analysis, both quantitative and qualitative, they determined that "[W]hat emerges clearly from this review is the unpalatable truth that 'normal' women can kill their children when they are confronted by social and economic circumstances which are severe enough."[46] They assert that attention should now be focused on the cultural factors that underpin the phenomenon of infanticide. The authors note that women bear an inordinate proportion of child care responsibilities, economic distress, and social isolation as parents. They suggest that neonaticide is deeply rooted in the dominant social constructions around womanhood and motherhood, and that the route to preventing this crime lies in working to restructure the conceptual frameworks about women.

A final theme pertaining to many of the young neonaticidal mothers is sexuality and one's perception of this aspect of identity. Bonnet[47] conducted a study in France with twenty-two women who had concealed their pregnancies. She discovered that when they found out they were pregnant, many of them had unpleasant recollections of sexuality, both from their childhoods and as adults. She reported that 20 percent of her sample had a history of physical or sexual abuse. This topic merits future inquiry as it may point the way to important long-term preventive strategies. For example, timely medical and psychological treatment of childhood abuse survivors may help to prevent involvement in later maladaptive behaviors.

Societal Responses to Neonaticide

The communitywide condemnation and cultural horror with which we react to such cases ultimately becomes integrally related to the way in which they are handled by the American judicial system. Even when our penal system is considered as a whole, we as a culture remain undecided at best, and bitterly divided at worst, about whether its focus should be to rehabilitate or to punish. Nowhere is this as clear as when we consider the vast array of charges, convictions, and prison sentences brought against neonaticidal women. In contrast to the United States, which has no unified means of punishing neonaticide, Britain has a specific statute governing such cases. The Infanticide Act was initially passed in 1922 and updated in 1938.[48] The basic premise behind this law is that women who commit neonaticide are likely to be mentally affected by the aftereffects of childbirth and/or lactation. Therefore, no charge higher than manslaughter can be brought against them. While the act's de facto pathologizing of childbirth is problematic, it is important to consider the mental status of a woman who expended her energy during nine months concealing her pregnancy from much, if not all, of the outside world.[49] Recent American law reviews have advocated that the United States consider adopting a similar approach to that used in England.[50]

The experiences of the women in our sample reflect the incoherence of the U.S. criminal justice system's response to neonaticide: some were charged with no crime at all and others with first-degree murder. The women also stood accused of other criminal charges, including child abuse, negligent homicide, second-degree murder, felony child endangerment, involuntary manslaughter, negligent manslaughter, and abuse of a corpse. Likewise, when criminal charges were brought, the end results varied between outright acquittal to life imprisonment. Some women were required to participate in psychotherapy while others were asked to perform community service.

The case of Tonya Cheser from Jefferson County, Kentucky, is particularly instructive on the issue of the range of options considered by courts. Though initially charged with murder, she was later convicted of first-degree manslaughter. She was sentenced to one year of incarceration followed by five years of "intensive" probation. Furthermore, she was to be allowed out of prison frequently in order to complete four hundred hours of community service, mental health counseling, periodic drug testing, and vocational training.[51]

Compounding the inconcistent nature of the U.S. response to neonaticide is the question of whether teenage girls should be charged and tried as adults. Generally, our legal system gives courts discretion as to when and whether to try juveniles as adults, as opposed to handing them over to juvenile court. The latter option carries with it the promise of a focus on rehabilitating the youthful offender in order to reintegrate her into society when she attains majority. More often than not, however, minors accused of neonaticide are tried as adults. Viewing them solely as perpetrators of murder, as opposed to frightened and overwhelmed young people who made a series of poor choices, can lead to a harsh set of judgments about them. Prominent mental health practitioners have made strong arguments both in favor of and in opposition to harsh criminal sentencing.[52] This struggle was particularly acute in the state of Ohio's case against Rebecca Hopfer. She was ultimately charged and tried as an adult after the judge determined that it was unlikely that Rebecca could be rehabilitated by the age of twenty-one (she was seventeen when she committed neonaticide). Rebecca is now serving a sentence of fifteen years to life at the Ohio Reformatory for Women.

When they are tried as adults for the crime of neonaticide, on the whole younger defendants fare better than older ones in terms of length of sentence. Among Schwartz and Isser's[53] sample, 22 women were above the age of nineteen and 22 were younger. Of the women in the older category, 15 were given sentences of five or more years, while among the younger women, only 10 were given such sentences. The correlation between age and sentencing is an area that requires further study in the future.

More study is also necessary to determine geographic variations in sentencing trends. Preliminary analyses reveal that some trends appear to exist. For example, ten neonaticide cases from California were examined in Schwartz and Isser's research. Of these, outcomes were only known for five—one was 14 years to life, two were 15 years to life, and two were 25 years to life. These results suggest that California was, by far, the state with the most consistent pattern of harsh sentencing in neonaticide cases. Louisiana and Pennsylvania had fewer cases, but also revealed relatively extreme sentences (i.e., 45 years and life). Illinois had the greatest range of imposed sentences (i.e., 90 days through 58 years), and New York appeared to be the most lenient (i.e., 8 months through 1.75 years).

Finally, one of the challenges to those seeking to defend women who commit neonaticide lies in educating the criminal justice officials concerned about the underlying mental state of such women during their pregnancies and at the time of their infants' births and deaths. In an effort to describe these factors, some within the legal and medical communities have proposed recognizing a "neonaticide syndrome."[54] In a 1996 legal case,[55] the defense offered to present expert testimony regarding such a syndrome. However, the judge excluded this testimony on the grounds that this syndrome is not a generally or widely accepted condition in the medical community.[56]

Preventing Neonaticide—Better Solutions

As noted previously, neonaticidal behavior is often influenced by relatively intangible factors such as emotional isolation and a perceived lack of resources, rather than by stereotypical indicators such as race or financial standing. However, it is critical to note the role played by existing healthcare services in limiting the incidence of contemporary neonaticide. Specifically, Pitt and Bale's review of the literature led them to state, "Evidence suggests that a relationship exists between the availability of abortion and neonaticide."[57] In other words, regions with limited abortion access for pregnant women have higher rates of neonaticide than do other areas. Lester found that rates of neonaticide were lower in the ten years following *Roe v. Wade* than in the ten years preceding the landmark case.[58] However, he found that there was not a significant correlation between rate of legal abortions and neonaticide.[59]

Although abortion remains legal in the United States at present, we must note the barriers that limit pregnant women's access to this service. First, there are geographic barriers to accessing abortion. Only 17 percent of all U.S. counties offer abortion services.[60] This means that most pregnant women must travel, and often over very long distances, in order to obtain an abortion. This fact has particularly harsh implications for teenagers seeking to preserve confidentiality, as transportation may be difficult to obtain and the distance traveled could require a long absence from home.

Laws requiring parental notification before minors can obtain abortions may constitute an additional barrier for young women. At present, thirty-two states require such notification.[61] There are numerous reasons why a young woman may wish to avoid telling her parents about her desire to terminate an unwanted pregnancy—shame, fear, a history of physical abuse, and even incest. Parental notification laws, particularly to the extent that they are misunderstood as requiring consent, may discourage the young woman from obtaining an abortion. Delaying the decision to act may not only complicate matters, but will also eventually render a later abortion too costly, too dangerous, and/or illegal.

The political fervor in the United States surrounding a woman's right to choose how to handle her pregnancy remains as heated and divisive today as it did when *Roe v. Wade* was tried in 1973. As such, there is a de facto barrier to accessing abortion in a climate in which protesters are likely to line the walk to the clinic. Although the U.S. Supreme Court has ruled that protesters may not block access to abortion clinics, there is no doubt that access to abortion is complicated by the fact that in order to gain access one must pass lines of protesters holding posters of fetuses and screaming accusations at those who enter the clinics. This is even more intimidating for the relatively young, immature woman who lacks a supportive network of family and friends. We live in a society in which abortion is legal, but infanticide remains an unthinkably horrible crime. Given this fact, we stress the importance of access to safe, affordable, and private abortions. This is an issue that affects not only childbearing women, but all the people who care about them. If increased options would help bring the number of neonaticides down, then this is one more consideration that should be taken into account when advocating reliable and safe access to abortion.

Physicians' awareness of their female patients' pregnancy status is another important issue. Several of the women we studied reported that their physicians did not notice their conditions while they were in their offices for other matters. Physician acknowledgment of pregnancy could very well be a crucial turning point in encouraging a young woman to take a more proactive attitude toward her situation. Discussions could be held about the importance of prenatal care and options regarding the pregnancy (e.g., abortion, adoption, caring for the child after birth, and the like). Furthermore, if physicians were educated about the dynamics of neonaticide they may discuss pregnancy with their young female patients more candidly.

Along these lines, Bourget and Labelle[62] suggest that timely detection and treatment of mental illness could reduce infanticide rates. The availability of mental health practitioners within medical settings would greatly facilitate this course of action. While it is well-documented that neonaticidal women are not likely to have a psychiatric diagnosis, personality dynamics related to maturity and identity development could be screened by available mental health practitioners, should the treating physician suspect that this may be necessary.

One solution that healthcare providers may want to consider is asking all young female patients (e.g., between the ages of eleven and twenty-five) whether they wish to be tested for pregnancy. Testing would be done only with the woman's consent and with an explanation given as to why it was recommended. Additionally, family members of teenagers should not be in the room when their daughters are being treated. This will permit the teenage patient to speak more freely about sensitive matters. Such measures might have drastically altered what was later to happen to Amy Grossberg. She visited her doctor four months into her pregnancy. With her mother present, she told her physician that she had been menstruating regularly. It later emerged that she had been purposely deceptive because she feared her mother's reaction. Medical students and residents should be trained early in their careers to treat teenage patients alone, and to ask them direct questions about their sexuality and reproductive healthcare needs. This may prove to be one means by which we can lower our nation's overall rates of neonaticide.

Just as physicians should be encouraged to alter the parameters of their practice with young female patients, so too is there a need to examine how religious institutions can better handle and tolerate women who unexpectedly become pregnant. Several of the women studied, across different religious faiths, reported that they did not seek out abortions when they discovered they were pregnant because they felt it was against their religious principles to do so. However, as their pregnancies progressed, they were unable to come up with viable solutions for their plight. Faced with limited options and a deep sense of shame, they ultimately resorted to neonaticide. Karen Dobrzelecki, age twenty, gave birth alone and subsequently tied an Easter ribbon around her son's throat and placed him in her bedroom closet. Her actions were discovered after she sought out medical care and reported to staff that she had given her newborn up for adoption. When confirmation could not be ascertained, legal authorities were summoned. Newspaper accounts of her trial consistently noted Karen's references to her devout Roman Catholicism as her primary deterrent to undergoing an abortion. She eventually pled guilty to involuntary manslaughter and was sentenced to thirteen years in prison.

Although this is not a call for religious institutions to embrace and advocate abortion as an alternative to unwanted pregnancy, it is critical that these institutions enter into dialogue with their young female parishioners. Hopefully, such conversations will be guided by the principle that women in all stages of life should feel empowered to make decisions that best suit their lives while also exhibiting their faith in and respect for a higher power. Only through such dialogue can potentially life-altering and life-damaging secrets be openly discussed and solutions be generated, such that all parties feel at peace with the rules of humans, nature, and God.

As noted previously, women who commit neonaticide range greatly in age. However, twenty of the thirty-seven women we studied were still in their teenage years. This statistic lends credence to the belief that schools can be powerful sources of education and intervention. Although the appropriateness of teaching sex education in schools is controversial, recent polls have shown that a majority of parents across the country favor such didactic offerings.[63] Open discussion about sex and sexuality remains fairly taboo in most American culture, which stance often leads teenagers to conceptually compartmentalize their sexual identities. While they are exploring this aspect of themselves, they may also feel compelled to be secretive about their conflicting feelings and experiences. For example, it may be very difficult to comfortably come to terms with simultaneous feelings of both shame and pride and fear and pleasure. Such confusion may impede teens from seeking out people and/or information that could help them obtain accurate information or sort through their feelings. If schools are able to freely offer resources or to make available trusted adults willing to discuss such matters with the students, such intense feelings may be better and more safely worked through.

Once again, we are calling on educational systems to look at how best to serve their students. Discussions should include all pertinent information, such as accurate information about sex, the possible repercussions of sex, and the benefits of both safe sex and abstinence. When armed with the most comprehensive and accurate information, as a society we can be more secure knowing that each young adult will eventually make a decision best suited to his or her beliefs and moral codes.

Mental health professionals and advocates can also advance the treatment of neonaticidal women by clarifying diagnostic conceptualizations of them. Kaplan and Grotowski[64] have advocated that the next edition of the DSM should include the diagnosis "Adjustment Disorder with Maladaptive Denial of a Physical Condition."[65] This suggestion may be the best preliminary step toward conceptualizing why women come to commit neonaticide. Thinking of the neonaticidal woman's act through this lens then allows us to consider how to provide help instead of punishment. Though some may argue that it is remiss not to treat neonaticidal women harshly, a strong argument can also be made that our nation's uneven and unfocused handling of these women thus far reveals our profound uncertainty regarding the extent to which they are blameworthy.

Individual citizens and communities have been so dismayed by the number of neonaticide cases that have been occurring nationally that initiatives to bring about change have begun to coalesce. The ABC news magazine program *20/20* devoted an entire edition to this topic in August 2000. It profiled Debi Faris,[66] a woman from Los Angeles who has made it her personal mission to commemorate the children who have been victims of neonaticide. She has created "The Garden of Angels" and in four years has organized forty-one burials of newborns. Other community-based programs were also featured on this edition of *20/20*.

There has been a concerted effort in Pittsburgh to provide women with alternatives to neonaticide. Baskets have been placed on the front porches of many homes in the hope that a desperate mother would leave her newborn there instead of taking fatal measures. As of the airing of the program, no child had ever been left in any of these baskets. Another initiative that has received attention lately are anonymous drop-offs.[67] Thirteen states have passed ordinances that allow women to drop their newborns off at designated locations with no questions asked or without any officials of the law present. It is too soon to know whether this measure will meet with any degree of success. Finally, *People Magazine*[68] described a twenty-four-hour telephone hot line in California that is available to mothers who do not want their newborns.

In thinking about the prevention of neonaticide, it is important to point out once again that neonaticide is rarely a premeditated act. Instead, it is an act born of panic and terror. Therefore, it seems somewhat unlikely that drop-off boxes will be a viable alternative for many young women. In fact it may very well lead to further stigmatization. As such, the focus on detecting pregnancy and preventing neonaticide remains of critical importance. As noted earlier, the biopsychosociocultural perspective may aid advocates and professionals from a number of different disciplines (e.g., medicine, psychology, law, sociology, and social work) to better understand and ultimately alter the face of neonaticide. A fundamental principle behind such a framework is that we can neither judge nor appropriately help a woman who commits neonaticide without understanding her background and the factors that motivated her action. Armed with a better understanding of the biological, psychological, sociological, and cultural factors that shape the actions of neonaticidal women, we can finally begin to articulate means of preventing these terrible tragedies from occurring.

Conclusion

Hundreds of neonaticides occur each year, damaging and destroying countless lives. Ostensibly happy families are exposed as shams, and young women who feared nothing so much as change find their lives irrevocably altered. Societal institutions and the professionals who run them have failed to acknowledge the patterned nature of this phenomenon, and have sought instead to haphazardly blame such crimes solely on the individuals who commit them. The time has come to take stock of what we already know about neonaticide and to begin to tailor meaningful options designed to identify and reach out to vulnerable and isolated pregnant women. In the meantime, the criminal justice system must reconsider its handling of the women who commit such terrible acts of desperation. Our response should be that of a civilized nation which recognizes that these cases find us with blood on all our hands, not just those of the young women most directly involved.

3

PURPOSEFUL KILLING

Neither "Mad" nor "Bad"

❏

There are a few cases of maternal filicide which have become infamous. One of them is that of Susan Smith. Although many people forget her name, few forget the basic facts. On October 25, 1994, Smith reported that a black man had stolen her car with her two children, Michael, three, and Alex, fourteen months, inside. For nine days Union, South Carolina, searched in vain for the boys. Finally, Smith confessed she had strapped the boys in their car seats, driven to a local lake, and rolled the car into the lake. Smith indicated that she had intended to kill herself and the boys but changed her mind at the last minute. She had considered killing just herself, but did not want to leave the boys without a mother.

Smith attempted numerous times to plead guilty to murder in exchange for a life sentence, but the prosecutor insisted on a trial. At her trial it became clear that Smith had had a tumultuous life, including her father's suicide when she was six years old, molestation by her stepfather, a history of depression, suicide, and substance abuse, and a failed marriage in the course of which both she and her husband had committed adultery. At the trial, she was portrayed as either a manipulative woman or an emotionally damaged adolescent. The jury deliberated only two and a half hours before finding her guilty. They deliberated approximately the same length of time and voted to spare her the death penalty.[1]

No one, not even Smith, disputed the fact that she had purposely killed her children. This distinguishes her from the women in the abuse-related and neglect categories who did not *purposely* kill their children. While some women in the assisted/coerced chapter purposely killed their children, the addition of a partner/accomplice distinguishes them from the women highlighted in this chapter. Although women in the neonaticide category may or may not have purposely killed their children, they have the distinction of completing the act within twenty-four hours postpartum, when there are a myriad of other factors which can influence behavior, including hormones. Additionally, the neonaticidal women often denied their pregnancy from the outset.

However, Smith and most of the other women assigned to this purposeful category did not deny the existence of their children, and were quite removed from any postpartum effects. This leads to speculation as to why and how these women were capable of committing such heinous acts. Generally, two lay theories are proposed: the mother must be "mad or bad."

"Mad or Bad"

Women portrayed as "mad" have been characterized as morally "pure" women who by all accounts have conformed to traditional gender roles and notions of femininity. These women are often viewed as "good mothers," and their crimes are considered irrational, uncontrollable acts, usually the direct result of a mental illness.[2] In contrast, women characterized as "bad" are seen as the complete antithesis of the "mad" woman. They are depicted as cold, callous, evil mothers who have often been neglectful of their children or their domestic responsibilities. Viewed as not having conformed to societal standards of "proper" female behavior, these mothers are often portrayed as sexually promiscuous, nonremorseful, and even nonfeminine.[3]

At first this appears to be a dichotomy—one is either "mad" or "bad." For example, most opinions surrounding the Susan Smith case argued that to be able to commit such a heinous crime she had to be either mentally unstable or evil. In fact, when we initially examined cases in the purposeful category, they seemed to line up under one of these two explanations, which we called purposeful filicide with mental illness and purposeful filicide without mental illness. But when we tried to create definitions for these subcategories, we found we would first have to determine whether to define mental illness using legal standards, mental health standards, or societal/cultural standards, and the dichotomy became meaningless.

In the legal arena, when the mental status of a defendant comes into question, it generally relates either to the person's competence to stand trial, or to the defendant's mental state at the time of the offense. Competence can be an issue at any stage of the criminal process, from arrest to sentencing. However, the most frequently adjudicated competence issue pertains to competence to stand trial. The standard for competence to stand trial is whether the defendant "has sufficient present ability to consult with his attorney with a reasonable degree of rational understanding and a rational as well as factual understanding of proceedings against him."[4] In other words, a defendant must understand the charges against her and the proceedings, so as to be able to aid her attorney in her defense. Susan Smith's competency was evaluated and she was found competent to stand trial. Although competency issues arise in the purposeful filicide cases, mental status issues are more commonly at stake.

Mental status at the time of the offense relates to a defendant's plea regarding her mental capacities when she committed the offense. The most frequently used plea relating to mental status at the time of the offense is, of course, the insanity defense. Each state fashions its own definition or test for insanity. However, a common test for insanity is some variant of the M'Naghten test. The M'Naghten test states, in part, that "To establish a defense on the ground of insanity, it must be clearly proved that, at the time of the committing of the act, the party accused was laboring under such a defect of reason, from disease of the mind, as not to know the nature and quality of the act he was doing; or, if he did know it, that he did not know what he was doing was wrong."[5]

Arguably, even the most psychotic of individuals knows what she is doing is wrong. The pivotal question, then, involves interpreting what it means to know the "nature and quality" of one's actions. Wisconsin used a variant of the M'Naghten test and found Jeffrey Dahmer, a man who killed numerous victims and then consumed some of their body parts, to be sane. Undoubtedly, using the same criteria Susan Smith would also be considered sane.[6] She knew what she was doing was wrong and if Dahmer knew the nature and quality of his acts, it would be hard to argue Smith did not. However, Smith did not plead insanity.

In order to aid jurors to better understand the mental capacities of the defendant and the insanity test used by the state, both prosecution and defense attorneys usually hire mental health experts. This brings definitions of mental illness used by mental health professionals into the legal arena. Unlike the dichotomous legal system in which an individual is either sane or insane, mental health professions use the *Diagnostic and Statistical Manual of Mental Disorders,* fourth edition (*DSM-IV*) to outline an array of illnesses with specific diagnostic criteria for each one, many of which could apply to mothers who purposely kill their children. Broadly defined, the disorders fall into two domains, clinical disorders and personality disorders.[7] Clinical disorders include diagnoses such as depression disorders, anxiety, and substance abuse disorders. A personality disorder is an "enduring pattern of inner experience and behavior that deviates markedly from the expectations of an individual's culture, is pervasive and inflexible, has an onset in adolescence or early adulthood, is stable over time, and leads to distress or impairment."[8]

Three personality disorders which might be particularly applicable to mothers who kill their children are dependent, antisocial, and borderline personality disorder. Dependent personality disorder is described as "a pattern of submissive and clinging behavior related to an excessive need to be taken care of."[9] Antisocial personality disorder is described as "a pattern of disregard for, and violation of, the rights of others."[10] Borderline personality disorder's main features include "a pattern of instability in interpersonal relationships, self-image, and affects, and marked impulsivity."[11]

Would Susan Smith have had a mental illness, according to the *DSM-IV*? We did not interview Susan Smith but read numerous books and accounts of her behavior. Clearly, she was and had been depressed and suicidal most of her life. She was likely grappling with depression the day she killed her children and has continued to grapple with it in prison following their murder. She has been on multiple suicide watches. She would certainly meet the criteria for at least one clinical disorder, depression. However, by all accounts Susan also had some features of a dependent personality disorder, including a history of an excessive need to be taken care of and fears of separation.

Although Susan Smith may have met the criteria for mental illness, that obviously would not satisfy legal standards for insanity and may have no bearing on competence at all. If everyone who had a mental illness as defined by the *DSM-IV* were able to successfully claim insanity or incompetence, it would likely encompass most criminals.

Clearly, the jury considered Susan Smith's mental health as a mitigating factor, but it is unclear as to whether that was because of expert testimony or societal definitions of insanity. One juror commented, "We all felt like Susan was a really disturbed person. . . . Giving her the death penalty wouldn't serve justice."[12] However, a "really disturbed person" is not a diagnosis in the *DSM-IV*, which suggests that the jurors considered not only the testimony of mental health experts in sparing Smith the death penalty, but societal beliefs and their own conventional wisdom regarding mental illness as well.

Definitional Dilemma

It became clear that there was no way we could create exact definitions of purposeful filicide with mental illness and purposeful filicide without mental illness. In fact, purposeful filicide appeared to be a continuum, not a dichotomy, with many exceptions and no rules. For example, if the mother had demonstrated signs of mental illness in the past but not at the time of the murder, would she represent purposeful filicide with or without mental illness? Or if the mother had no history of mental illness but attempted or successfully committed murder-suicide, would this be considered purposeful filicide with or without mental illness? What if she committed suicide for cultural reasons or for altruistic reasons such as wanting to spare the child what she believed would be a life of abuse? What if the woman was suffering from a disorder such as postpartum psychosis, which is not a recognized mental disorder in the *DSM-IV*? Although she appeared to have a mental disorder there could be no diagnosis.

We finally decided not to try and distinguish between the cases on the basis of mental illness but to include them all under a category known as purposeful filicide. In order to highlight the complexity of the issue, in this chapter we will first examine some of the purposeful cases in detail and then interpret them using various frameworks, such as legal, psychological, and sociocultural. Next, the overarching themes and patterns that emerged from our purposeful filicide cases will be outlined, followed by their social and policy implications.

Purposeful Filicide Cases Illustrating the Definitional Dilemma

Debora Green

In high school, Debora Green was a cheerleader and covaledictorian of her class. She excelled in college and medical school, specializing in oncology. She married

Michael Ferrar, who was also in medical school and later became a cardiologist. By 1995, they had three children, Tim, thirteen, Kate, ten, and Kelly, six, and lived in an affluent Kansas City suburb. Debora had quit her practice to stay home with the children. By all appearances the family had everything. However, the couple had struggled with marital problems for years. Michael was involved in a relationship with another woman and, in July, he told Debora he wanted a divorce. In September, Michael attempted to have Debora involuntarily committed to a mental hospital because he thought she was abusing alcohol and was also a suicide risk. Instead, Green voluntarily admitted herself to a different hospital, was prescribed antidepressant and antianxiety medications, and was discharged after four days.

On the night of October 23, 1995, Michael and Debora had an argument on the phone and Michael threatened to take the children from her. He also told her he thought she was crazy. Just before midnight, the house in which Debora and the children were living in erupted in flames. Tim and Kelly perished. Kate jumped to safety. On Thanksgiving eve, Debora was charged with the murders of Tim and Kelly and the attempted murder of Michael and Kate. Michael alleged Debora had been poisoning him with castor seeds since August. Michael nearly died from complications resulting from poisonings. In 1996, when Debora was scheduled to go to trial, her competence was assessed, and she was found competent to stand trial. In April, Debora pled no contest to the charges and was eventually sentenced to forty years without parole.[13] A portion of the statement she made at her sentencing hearing follows:

> *The death of a child—any child, under any circumstances—is a terrible human tragedy. The death of these children, under these circumstances, is a tragedy almost too great to bear. It is, nevertheless, a tragedy that I must bear for the rest of my life, and one for which I must also bear responsibility. Nothing that I can do, or that can be done to me, can bring my children back. In accepting responsibility for this crime, I recognize that I must face and accept the punishment assessed by the court. I must also face the sorrow of the loss of my children, and the reality of my role in their death. . . . Alcohol, psychiatric illness, and even more basic communication failures within our family set the stage for this tragedy. . . .*

*My desire in taking this course of action {pleading no contest} is to spare
Kate and the rest of my family any further trauma.*[14]

Green was later interviewed by Ann Rule and her story was the subject
of the book *Bitter Harvest*. In January 2000, Green attempted to with-
draw her pleas, claiming she had not been mentally competent to make
the pleas when she entered them and had been unduly influenced by her
attorneys. She eventually filed a motion for a new trial, but withdrew
that motion when the prosecutor indicated he would seek the death
penalty.

A month before the fatal fire, Green's husband thought she was so
mentally ill that she needed to be involuntarily committed. After a
short hospital stay, she was discharged with an arsenal of psychotropic
medications to fight her depression and anxiety. In general, psychotropic medications control the symptoms of mental illness but do not
treat the illness. How then did Debora Green overcome her illness in the
month between her hospitalization and the fire? During that month she
also continued to drink alcohol, which her physicians warned could
react negatively with the medications and would seem to have exacerbated her symptoms. After her arrest, Green received no substantive
treatment and was coping with the loss of her children and facing a possible death sentence, factors which could hardly have enhanced her stability. Nevertheless the court found Green competent to stand trial and
since she did not plead insanity, her mental status at the time of the offense was not discussed.

Green clearly would meet the criteria for several clinical diagnoses.
However, if Green purposely killed her children and did not have a recent history of mental health treatment, she still would likely have an
antisocial personality disorder. Therefore, according to psychological
definitions, Green would clearly have had a mental illness. Green's case
illustrates one aspect of the dilemma inherent in the dichotomy of "mad
versus bad." In Green's case, it is even further complicated by the fact
that she was charged with two different crimes: murder and attempted

murder. If the murders were impulsive acts, they could be construed as the product of mental illness. However, the prolonged poisoning of her husband would seem more calculated and less the product of illness. Given that Green is guilty of committing these crimes, the only thing that is clear is that she purposely committed them.

Kimberlee Snyder

Like many expectant mothers, twenty-five-year-old Kimberlee Snyder was ecstatic about the prospect of having her first child. In the months leading up to the birth, she spent countless hours shopping for baby clothes and pouring over books on pregnancy and motherhood. So when her daughter Tahlor Dawn was born, she and her husband couldn't have been happier about the new addition to their family. However, no one could have been prepared for the events that unfolded five months later, when on July 30, 1996, Kimberlee Snyder killed her child in a fit of rage.

On the day of the murder, Snyder awoke in what she claims was an agitated state and began hitting and shaking Tahlor Dawn when she started making noises like she was unhappy. After shoving a baby bottle into her mouth until she bled, she began slapping her in the face, leaving impression marks on her forehead. She then carried her into the bathroom, where she attempted to tend to the marks on her head. The assault eventually continued as Snyder violently threw Tahlor Dawn onto the bathroom floor.

Snyder explained that she felt like she was having an out of body experience and like a demon had taken over her body. When she realized what she had done, Snyder called 911, claiming her daughter had fallen from the kitchen counter. Five-month old Tahlor Dawn suffered massive head injuries and died the next day after being removed from life support systems. At her trial, Snyder's attorneys argued that she was not a premeditated murderer, but rather a woman who suffered a psychotic episode brought on by postpartum depression.[15]

Postpartum disorder is the term used to refer to several disorders mothers experience after giving birth. The disorders range in severity from postpartum blues to postpartum depression to postpartum psychosis.

Postpartum blues include symptoms such as tearfulness, headaches, irritability, and appetite changes, which are common experiences for women in the postpartum period. In fact, approximately 85 percent of new mothers experience some form of depressed mood within the first two weeks of giving birth. However, the symptoms generally dissipate within two weeks to three months postpartum and rarely, if ever, result in infanticide.[16]

In certain instances, more severe forms of postpartum blues can develop, such as the postpartum depression that Kimberlee Snyder apparently experienced. Affecting between 5 to 20 percent of new mothers, postpartum depression usually develops within the first six months after birth, with symptoms characterized by tearfulness, irritability, and intense feelings of inadequacy and anxiety relating to one's ability to care for the baby.[17] In very rare cases, postpartum depression can lead to postpartum psychosis (occurring in only 1 to 2 per 1,000 births), where mothers experience hallucinations, delusions, obsessional thinking, and feelings of hopelessness.[18]

Only one month after giving birth, signs were already emerging that Snyder was suffering from postpartum depression. During a routine follow-up examination, Snyder told a midwife that she had feelings of anger toward her daughter and resented not having time for herself. The midwife, suspecting Snyder might be suffering from postpartum depression, referred her to a psychiatrist for further evaluation. Upon examination, the psychiatrist prescribed antidepressant medication after noting that Snyder had several indicators of postpartum depression.[19]

It seems apparent from both the midwife and psychiatrist's actions that they believed Snyder to be suffering from postpartum depression. However, she did not receive an official diagnosis because there is little recognition of postpartum syndromes within the mental health field. The *DSM-IV* does not recognize postpartum depression or postpartum psychosis as separate disorders. Instead, they are subsumed under the broader category of depression or as a generic and poorly defined form of psychosis (i.e., Psychotic Disorder Not Otherwise Specified).[20] So

Kimberlee Snyder was not diagnosed at all, and nine days after being prescribed antidepressant medication, she told the psychiatrist she was feeling better and never contacted him again for further treatment. Four months later, Tahlor Dawn was dead.

Although postpartum depression is not an officially recognized mental disorder, Snyder pled not guilty by reason of insanity to charges of murder, involuntary manslaughter, and child endangering. Her defense was based solely on the claim that she was suffering from a severe form of postpartum depression at the time of her baby's death, giving her the distinction of being the first woman in the state of Ohio to use postpartum depression as an insanity defense.

According to Ohio law, a person is said to be not guilty by reason of insanity if, because of a mental disease or defect, she was unable to determine the wrongfulness of her act. Both the defense and prosecution called in psychiatrists who gave opposing testimony as to Snyder's mental state at the time of the death. Prosecution psychiatrists testified that Snyder was not suffering from depression at the time of the incident and did not suffer from a mental disorder or defect. The prosecution also refuted the midwife's suspicions of postpartum depression, claiming her diagnosis was an unscientific finding based solely on her previous experience in identifying women at risk.[21]

Snyder testified during her trial that only two weeks after her daughter was born, she started to have feelings about wanting to harm her baby. She indicated, however, that she kept those feelings a secret because she was ashamed and did not want anyone to think that she was a bad mother. Since Snyder elected a bench trial, a judge was left to sort through the contradictory expert testimony. Although Snyder presented compelling evidence to the court, she was found guilty of murder. However, the judge stepped down before sentencing her. Snyder pled guilty to involuntary manslaughter and child endangering to avoid a retrial and conviction carrying a possible sentence of life in prison. She was sentenced to fifteen years in prison.[22]

Snyder did not have a diagnosable mental illness and was not found to be insane by an Ohio judge using Ohio law. It seems clear, however, that she was suffering from postpartum depressive symptoms, as evidenced by her psychiatrist's decision to prescribe antidepressant medication. Yet during her trial, prosecutors attempted to portray Snyder as an uncaring mother who was disappointed that she had given birth to a girl instead of a boy.

Is it possible that the court held maternal biases against Snyder which ultimately led to her conviction? Snyder's statement that she was reluctant to publicly disclose the negative feelings she had toward her child because she did not want anyone to think she was a bad mother, are typical of most women suffering from postpartum disorders. These sentiments may reflect social constructions of motherhood, which often place extreme demands and pressures on women who experience negative feelings toward their newborns.

In general, society views women as innate nurturers who are expected to remain joyful and happy during their pregnancy and throughout motherhood. Consequently, when new mothers like Snyder experience negative emotions they often suffer in silence, coping with the shame and guilt that often accompany such feelings.[23] Given the fact that Snyder developed an atypical form of depression not recognized by the *DSM-IV* and she was found not to be insane under Ohio law, it remains unclear whether she should ultimately be determined "mad" or "bad." What seems clear, however, is that throughout her pregnancy and before the onset of her symptoms, Snyder was a dutiful and attentive mother who clearly loved her child. Yet at the same time, she also purposely killed her in a fit of rage.

Terri Lynn Esterak

"I'm sorry I had to do this to you and my Mom and my family . . . but I cannot go on with my life while my children suffer. I will not allow another day of

unhappiness to go before their eyes . . . to see them crying, begging, wondering why I left them, wondering why they can't be with me, to see their pain has become unbearable." [24]

These were the final words 31-year-old Terri Lynn Esterak wrote to her fiancé in a four-page suicide note, before taking a .38 caliber revolver, shooting and killing her three young daughters and then herself in August of 1994. She was embroiled in a bitter custody battle over her daughters, ages nine, four, and two. Her ex-husband had been granted primary custody and she was supposed to return them after a one-month visit. Instead Esterak, who believed her daughters did not want to go back to their father, and who was distraught over the prospect of leaving them, checked into a posh resort hotel and methodically shot each of her girls in the chest, before turning the gun on herself. [25]

Murder-suicides are perhaps the most difficult to classify in terms of the "mad" or "bad" dichotomy simply because the woman is not alive to tell her story. Cases involving suicide are generally accompanied by questions regarding the mental state of the individual at the time of the death. Add to that the unfathomable act of the murder of a child by their mother, and many will assume that she must have been suffering from a mental illness to have committed such a heinous act.

Based on the facts of the case, it appears that Terri Lynn Esterak was experiencing a great deal of emotional distress regarding the custody battle over her three daughters, and one can assume that she had been entertaining thoughts of suicide for some time prior to the deaths. However, there is no current mental disorder in the *DSM-IV* which lists suicidal thoughts or attempts as the sole criterion.

Additionally, there is no evidence that Esterak had a prior psychiatric history or that she was in counseling at the time of the murders. It is likely that she was experiencing symptoms characteristic of depression. However, these symptoms do not appear to have negatively impacted her daily functioning, as she had been able to adequately care for herself and her children during their one-month visit. Thus, it is questionable whether she would have met the criteria for a major depressive disorder according to the *DSM-IV* or that she would have met the legal requirement for insanity.

It seems difficult at best to categorize Esterak as "mad." It is evident that she was distraught at the thought of losing custody of her children and felt that she could no longer bear the pain of living without them. Nor does she appear to have been "bad." In her suicide note, Esterak expressed remorse for her actions and apologized to her family for the pain she was causing them, actions that seem incongruous for an evil woman without a conscience. In fact, her actions may even be considered altruistic. Since she had decided to take her own life, Esterak may have killed her children to spare them the anguish of growing up without her.

It is clear that Terri Lynn Esterak purposely killed her children and herself. However, if Esterak had lived to go to trial, the legal system would undoubtedly have found her to be sane.

Del Frances Bennett

Del Frances Bennett, a thirty-eight-year-old, single mother of three, had worked tirelessly to improve the lives of her children. She attended college, graduated, and eventually secured a job as a lab technician. However, her new job meant that she no longer met the requirements for public assistance, and she lost her Medicaid benefits, housing assistance, and food stamps. Additionally, she had been unsuccessful in receiving child support from her children's fathers and was struggling daily just to make ends meet. Neighbors and friends admitted she was frustrated and stressed and in a lengthy suicide note, Bennett indicated she was depressed and anxious about her financial situation. Ultimately, the mounting financial pressures took their toll and Del Frances Bennett fatally shot her three daughters, ages five, seven, and nine, set fire to her home, and then shot and killed herself.[26]

It seems clear that the economic pressures Del Frances Bennett was experiencing weighed heavily in her decision to end the lives of herself and her children. Like many mothers making the transition from welfare to work, the pride that comes from no longer needing public assistance is often tempered by the harsh realities of low-paying jobs and substandard or no health insurance. Coupled with the fact that she was not receiving financial support from the biological fathers of her children, it is not surprising that Bennett was experiencing anxiety and a high level of stress.

It is likely that she worried constantly about her ability to provide for herself and her daughters and feared for their futures. Bennett appeared to have been suffering from depression in the weeks and possibly months before the murders. However, there is no evidence that she was receiving any mental health services. Although Bennett may have met the *DSM-IV* criteria for a major depressive disorder, given her financial situation it is doubtful whether she would have been able to afford adequate mental health treatment.

Everyone who knew Del Frances Bennett reported that she was a loving and devoted mother who tried to do everything within her power to provide a better life for herself and her children. In fact, one week before the murders Bennett had agreed to tutor students in the same job training program that had assisted her in getting off welfare.[27] Thus, a convincing case cannot seem to be made for categorizing her as "bad."

Although Bennett had done everything society tells "welfare mothers" to do (i.e., get an education and secure a job), it had still not been enough to provide a financially stable home for her children. Consequently, she may have lost all hope and felt that murder-suicide was the only option she had left to spare her and her children from growing up poor with uncertain futures. Like Esterak, had Bennett lived to go to trial, she too would have likely been found to be sane.

Erika Arroyo

On September 4, 1998, Erika Arroyo, twenty-two, fed her son, Armando, a drug cocktail which she thought would kill him. An hour later when he awakened, she drowned the three-year-old in the bathtub. Several hours later she car-

ried his body to the local convenience store and called police indicating she had left the boy in the tub only to return and find him dead. Arroyo was arrested, confessed, and was charged with first-degree murder.

Early in 1998, Arroyo had moved to Denver from El Paso to take a job. She left behind her parents, a sister, and Armando's father. Erika reported that Armando's father had been abusive to the child. A few months after the move she began living with Cesar Barajas, a Mexican immigrant who spoke no English. Armando, Erika, and Cesar lived together as a family until Erika became pregnant. Erika traveled to El Paso, aborted the child, and upon returning to Denver told Barajas she was going to move back to El Paso. Apparently she relented but Barajas indicated he could no longer bear to raise another man's child as it would remind him of his own son who had been aborted. Barajas indicated Erika would have to choose between him and Armando. Erika contacted adoption agencies but became discouraged when she learned the biological father would have to agree to the adoption. Later Barajas claimed Erika killed Armando to prove her love for him. Arroyo maintained she killed him to save him from a life of abuse.[28]

In December 1998, Erika pled not guilty by reason of insanity and at least one psychiatrist agreed she was legally insane at the time of the killings. The judge ordered another psychiatric evaluation.[29] *In December 1999, Arroyo pled guilty to child abuse resulting in death and in February 2000 she was sentenced to a maximum of forty-eight years in prison.*[30]

Like all the other cases in this chapter, Arroyo purposely killed her child. Once again she does not fit neatly into the "mad versus bad" dichotomy. Clearly she may fit the criteria for some diagnoses, including depression or dependent personality disorder, and she may even have fit the legal criteria for insanity. However, even more compelling in this case are the social and cultural factors which must influence any determinations of sanity or insanity.

This was a woman who had few resources or supports. Her apartment was described as barren. Arroyo was being forced to make a decision between her son and her relationship, with no alternative solutions.

Adoption was not an option. If she sent Armando back to El Paso or she returned to El Paso with him, he and/or she would no doubt have been victims of the father's abuse. In some ways her choice represented a rational, logical response to an irrational, illogical situation. Does that make her "mad" or "bad"?

Ophilia Yip

Ophilia Yip, a thirty-four-year-old Chinese immigrant, was called a model parent by those who knew her. Others also say she was a woman who was severely depressed and preoccupied with the pressures of raising a family in Los Angeles. Suspecting she was distressed, her husband took her to see a counselor, but after the second session, she never returned. Yip told her husband that because of her Chinese upbringing and heritage, she felt she had a problem that only someone from her own culture could understand. Yip had also never completely assimilated into American culture and felt particularly isolated in Los Angeles, fearing that an urban setting was unhealthy for her children. So a few months after her visit to the counselor, and apparently plagued by a growing depression that had gone untreated, Ophilia Yip drowned herself and her four children, ages three, four, six, and thirteen by driving her van off a pier into the Los Angeles Harbor.[31]

It is apparent from the facts of the case that both Yip and her husband suspected she might have been depressed. Although they sought treatment for her depressive symptoms, Yip did not feel comfortable with the counselor and did not return for future sessions. Ophilia Yip was likely suffering from clinical depression and her case addresses some of the dilemmas encountered by immigrant women and other women from ethnically diverse backgrounds when they are faced with mental health issues.

Within the mental health field multilingual, culturally sensitive mental health services are lacking. Language barriers, as well as lack of knowledge regarding cultural differences surrounding the definition of mental illness, may prevent many women from ethnically diverse backgrounds from seeking help. Furthermore, those who do seek help, like Ophilia Yip, are often dissatisfied with the treatment they receive and do not return for follow-up care. As a result, they may never receive an appropriate diagnosis or treatment.

Yip may have believed that there was no help for her problem, viewing suicide as her only means to escape the pain of her depression. Additionally, Yip was growing more concerned about the welfare of her children growing up in a large city. Her decision to take their lives does not appear to be the action of a cold, callous woman, but that of a woman who may have believed that by killing them she would be protecting them from an unhealthy environment. However, would the legal system see her as insane? No.

Theresa Lynne Cheek

On the day of her son's death, Theresa Lynne Cheek told her husband she planned to get the devil out of him, but did not indicate that she would physically harm him. However, after her husband left for work, and in an apparent attempt to save him from what she thought would be eternal damnation, she killed her two-and-a-half-year-old son. When attempts to strangle him were unsuccessful, she stabbed him in the heart and then tried to set fire to his body to drive out the demons. Cheek was charged with aggravated murder, found to be not guilty by reason of insanity, and ordered to begin immediate treatment in a state forensic hospital.[32]

It is clear from the facts of this case that Cheek was suffering from a mental disorder, specifically a form of psychosis, when she murdered her son. Unlike other cases within this category, there was no dispute as to her mental state at the time of the death. Since she was found to be legally insane, this represents a classic case of the "mad" category. However, cases such as Cheek's are in the minority.

Ambiguities and variations in what constitutes mental illness make it impossible to classify most of the women in this category as mentally ill. However, it is clear that a significant number of them were struggling with emotional difficulties prior to the deaths. Many of the mothers in this category expressed feelings of hopelessness, despair, and suicidal thoughts prior to the killings, and several of them may have developed a depressive disorder when they killed their children.

Overall Findings

Several research methods were used to gather case information for this subtype, but limited data were available on some mothers in this group. Although we included them in our analysis, we were unable to obtain specific details for every factor we were interested in studying. However, the one salient feature linking these women together was that they had purposely killed their children.

Remarkably, despite the level of diversity between the cases and the paucity of available information in some instances, striking and clear patterns emerged when we reviewed the data.

Multiple Deaths

One of the most striking features of this category, which sets the women in this group apart from the other mothers discussed in this book, is the overwhelming number of cases involving multiple deaths of children. Nearly 39 percent of mothers within this category killed more than one child. When we consider cases of murder-suicide alone, the number jumps to a staggering 68 percent. Additionally, 16 percent of the cases involved serial deaths, in which the mother killed multiple children over an extended period.[33] Over half (57 percent) of the multiple deaths involved attempted or successful murder-suicides. This large percentage suggests that mothers who attempt suicide and then resort to infanticide pose a greater risk to all or the majority of their offspring.

Although we do not know conclusively why these mothers killed multiple children, the suicide notes left behind by some shed light on possible motives for the killings. Terri Lynn Esterak appears to have killed her children to spare them the pain of growing up without her. As for Del Frances Bennett, overwhelming financial pressures apparently led her to kill her daughters to protect them from a lifetime of poverty. The sentiments expressed by these women may be typical of other mothers who attempt to kill themselves and their children.

Finally, some of the mothers within this category may have killed multiple children to ensure there were no siblings left behind to mourn the deaths of their brothers or sisters.

Fire

In 37 percent of the cases involving multiple killings, mothers chose fire as the primary mode of death, setting fire to their homes or cars. In a few cases, they killed their children by some other means, such as a gunshot wound or drowning, and then in a final act set fire to their homes.

This phenomenon is unique to the mothers within the purposeful filicide category. Although several children in the neglect category were killed in fires, the majority of them set the fires as a direct result of their mother's negligence. In contrast, in cases of purposeful filicide, the mothers actually set the fires to cause their children's deaths.

Many of these mothers may have felt their lives were spiraling out of control. In their minds, the fire may have been a final attempt to exert some control over what had been an otherwise powerless existence. Since fires usually cause irreparable damage and considerable destruction, these women were able to destroy all tangible remains of their children's lives, and at the same time dictate how their bodies would be handled in death (i.e., no bodies remained to be physically handled nor could the bodies be buried).

Additionally, unlike other methods such as drowning or stabbing which require the mother to play an active role in the child's death, a fire is a far more passive method of killing. By setting fire to their homes or cars, these women could remove themselves from the scene of the crime without having to witness their children dying, possibly making the task easier to accomplish.

Failed Relationships

Close to 42 percent of women in this category had experienced a recent failed relationship, separation, or divorce prior to the murders. Additionally many women, such as Terri Lynn Esterak, were in the midst of bitter custody disputes when they killed their children.

The negative impact of a divorce has been well documented and it can be a very stressful event for an individual to endure.[34] However, the impact of a failed relationship may prove to be even more devastating for the women in this category for several reasons.

First, the majority of mothers within this category were married. With the exception of women in the assisted/coerced category, this characteristic appears to be unique to this subtype. For example, many of the women within the abuse-related, neglect, assisted/coerced, and neonaticide categories had either never been married, were in abusive relationships, or were not currently in relationships with the fathers of their children. Although women are remaining single for longer periods of time, there is still societal pressure on them to marry. Consequently, by divorcing or ending a relationship, many of these mothers may have felt they were violating a socially imposed gender norm. They may also have feared becoming single again, given their potentially decreased prospects for remarriage.

Additionally, many of them may have experienced some fear about the quality of their lives after their divorce. Studies have shown that divorce often has a greater negative financial impact on women than men, resulting in poorer living conditions and lifestyles.[35] As a result, they may have worried about their ability to provide for themselves in their husband's absence. Additionally, they may have feared losing custody of their children. All these fears could have contributed to their fatal decisions.

Devotion

At first glance, the mothers within this category seem like premeditated murderers who violently killed their children. However, upon deeper examination one of the most distinctive features of these women's stories was their devotion toward their children. While it may seem like an oxymoron to describe women who kill their children as loving mothers, by all accounts that is exactly what most of them were. The overwhelming majority of them had no history of abuse or neglect toward their children and most people who knew them spoke of their undying love for their kids.

Erika Arroyo did not have a history of abusing her son. In fact, she left her son's father, claiming he had abused the three-year-old. Additionally, neighbors and friends of both Del Frances Bennett and Terri Lynn Esterak remarked that they were both model parents. How then does an otherwise devoted mother end up killing her kids?

It is obvious that many of these women were extremely distressed at the time of the murders. For those mothers who attempted to commit suicide, they may have been unable to bear the thought of their children growing up without them. Thus their actions may have been motivated by an attempt to reunite the family in death.

Additionally, mothers like Erika Arroyo may have killed their children to spare them a life of future pain and may have viewed their act as the ultimate sacrifice. Erika Arroyo likely felt that her options were limited, as she was left with the agonizing choice of sending her child back to an abusive environment or losing her only source of economic and financial stability. In the end, by killing him she not only spared her son a life of future abuse, but sacrificed her own life as well, as she was eventually sentenced to forty-eight years in prison.

Cultural Issues

Culture and ethnicity played a significant role within this category, particularly as they related to immigrant women. A large number of immigrant women were represented, compared to the other subtypes discussed in the book.

Many immigrants face unique challenges when they move to the United States. Problems of acculturation, assimilation, as well as language barriers often make the adjustment to American life a difficult one. Although Ophilia Yip had lived in the United States for several years, she felt isolated in the American cultural environment.

Additionally, many immigrants face financial difficulties due to limited resources. As a result, they often find themselves struggling daily to provide their families with basic necessities. It is possible that the pressures of adjusting to a new culture, increased isolation, language barriers, as well as financial difficulties may have affected some of the immigrant women in this category, influencing their decision to end the lives of their children. Furthermore, the negative stigma attached to mental illness in some cultures may have made many of them reluctant to seek out mental health services.

Interventions

One of the most notable characteristics in this chapter was the large number of women who threatened, attempted, or successfully committed suicide. More than half the mothers within this category either attempted to or were successful in killing themselves as well as their children. While abuse and neglect and more recently, neonaticide, have become the focus of nationwide preventative efforts and current legislation, far less attention has been paid to mothers who not only kill their children but attempt to kill themselves as well.

Generally, the subject of suicide has remained taboo for many families and for much of society, and in cases in which the mothers have died, the motivation behind their decisions often remains a mystery. Additionally, several factors can contribute to a mother's decision to take her own life, making it increasingly difficult to identify reliable risk factors.

Based on our findings, women who commit infanticide and then attempt to take their own lives are more likely to kill multiple children, leaving many families at risk. Therefore, national suicide prevention organizations need to focus their research efforts on identifying risk factors. Additionally, suicide and crisis hotlines need to be made aware of this trend so they can screen for at-risk mothers and begin developing interventions to provide them with services.

In addition to suicide, failed relationships were also another significant trend, as a large number of women in this category were dealing with the aftermath of a recent divorce or failed relationship in the weeks and months prior to the murders of their children. The end of a relationship, particularly a marriage, is stressful for both parties. However, our findings suggest that the impact of a divorce may place some mothers at increased risk for infanticide.

While some divorces are amicable, many are not, as battles over custody, property, and child support can turn once loving partners into bitter enemies. In fact, several of the mothers in this chapter were in the midst of custody disputes at the time of their children's deaths. Unfortunately, the adversarial nature of the legal system often serves to increase the level of animosity between the two parties. Due to the apparent increased risk for infanticide during this critical time, a serious argument can be made for making changes in the adversarial nature of divorce litigation. Fortunately, more courts are turning to alternative dispute resolution (ADR) and mediation to resolve legal disputes. This may be one effective means of reducing the level of anxiety and stress that often accompanies a divorce.

Mediation may help eliminate the conflictual nature of the process, allowing both parties to make their cases in the presence of a neutral party. Doing so may lead to more amicable settlements which serve the best interests of both the parents and the children. In addition, the process may provide much needed emotional support. While not perfect, the use of mediation may provide a better alternative than the current system, which tends to breed more contempt than solutions.

Although a very small percentage of mothers within this category suffered from postpartum disorders (8 percent), prevention efforts can be easily implemented to substantially reduce such tragedies from occurring. Healthcare professionals should be informed about the more severe forms of postpartum syndromes (postpartum depression and postpartum psychosis), which, if undetected, pose a significant health risk for both mother and child, including child abuse, infanticide, and suicide. Armed with such knowledge, healthcare professionals should educate women and their families about postpartum disorders during their pregnancy, should encourage expectant mothers to discuss their feelings, screen women prenatally for risk factors, and provide referral sources to women and their families dealing with these disorders.[36]

As this chapter has revealed, the majority of these mothers did not seek treatment for any of the problems or emotional difficulties they were experiencing. The need for greater mental health intervention was highlighted in the statements Debora Green made at her sentencing hearing:

> Alcohol abuse, and the psychiatric problems that both lead to alcohol abuse and spring from it, are treatable diseases. They are not, however, diseases for which the afflicted person will readily seek help on their own. Many of you know in your own lives of people in danger from these illnesses. It is never easy to intervene in the life of another. I would ask that you look at these opportunities for intervention in your lives, and take the steps that must be taken to salvage those lives in danger, before it is too late, as it has become for me and my family.[37]

Summary

This chapter was born out of the initial challenges we encountered in attempting to classify women who purposely killed their children into two discrete categories: with mental illness and without mental illness. This proved to be an arduous task as we realized that these women did not easily fit into a dichotomy (i.e., "mad versus bad") but represented a diverse continuum, covering the entire spectrum of mental illness, ethnic and cultural group distinctions, and socioeconomic strata. Ultimately the "mad versus bad" dichotomy fails to accurately classify these mothers because it does not take into account the varying contextual, legal, and psychological factors which contributed to their emotional states and decisions to kill their children. However, although the women outlined in this chapter do not fit into discrete categories, when examining the data through a purely psychological lens, some general hypotheses can be made.

It is clear that the vast majority of the mothers were experiencing some form of emotional distress, although in varying degrees, at the time of the murders. In the weeks prior to her children's deaths, Ophilia Yip had grown increasingly concerned about their safety and Theresa Lynne Cheek feared that her son had become possessed by demons. Additionally, more than half the women in this chapter experienced suicidal thoughts, as evidenced by their attempts to kill themselves along with their children.

Although the majority of these women would not meet the legal requirement for insanity, their level of emotional distress (i.e., depressive symptoms, anxiety, and suicidal thoughts) suggests that most of them may have been suffering from disorders such as depression, anxiety, and psychosis. A much smaller group of mothers in this category appeared to exhibit symptoms characteristic of personality disorders.[38] For these women, the filicide may have been the culmination of long-standing patterns of relational dysfunction. For example, Debora Green showed signs of a possible antisocial personality

93

disorder, as evidenced by her elaborate plan and prolonged attempts to poison her husband.

We are not the first researchers to suggest that some filicidal mothers might have personality disorders.[39] d'Orban[40] noted that personality disorders represented the largest diagnostic category in his sample, and Bourget and Bradford[41] made a diagnosis of personality disorder in approximately half their cases. Generally, mothers who purposely kill their children are labeled "bad" and are depicted as cold, callous, and evil mothers who abused their children. An argument can be made that in a few cases the mothers simply wanted to kill their children and their actions were not mediated by mental illness. However, such mothers are in the minority and do not adequately represent the majority of cases we reviewed in our analysis.

Ultimately, no one knows which of these multiple factors contributed to these mothers' decisions to kill their children. However, our analysis reveals that emotional distress plays a significant role in many cases of purposeful filicide, in conjunction with other social variables.

4

MATERNAL NEGLECT

A Search for Meaning

❏

Tiffany Hickman

Tiffany Hickman, a twenty-one-year-old single mother, left her three-month-old daughter unattended in an infant tub that was placed in a larger bathtub, where her nineteen-month-old son was also bathing. Hickman then left the bathroom to prepare food for a Super Bowl party and answer a telephone call during which she argued with her son's father about finances. Police believe that she left the children unsupervised for approximately five minutes, and when she returned, she found her daughter floating face down in the water.

The year prior to the death, Hickman had been living in a 106-unit apartment building that offered a two-year transitional program for single-parent families which included parenting classes. In the past, she had been cited three times for child neglect, and had recently received one year's probation for locking her children in a bedroom while she was at a neighbor's home talking on the telephone. Hickman pled guilty to child abuse resulting in death and was sentenced to ten years in prison.

In several ways, Tiffany Hickman represents other mothers who have been imprisoned for killing their children through neglect. Hickman is a young mother who either disregarded or was unaware of bathing safety, and it cost her the life of her infant daughter. She is also a single mother handling the full responsibilities and stresses of parenting two children below the age of two. This usually means that any emotional resources she has have been depleted and that she has very little personal time. Like many women in this category, financial stress abounds for Hickman and she probably worries constantly about whether she can provide adequate food, housing, and clothing. These life circumstances sometimes lead to fatal child neglect and are realities for many women with children across this country.

Power and Privilege

Before elaborating upon the characteristics of mothers in the category of filicide due to neglect, it is essential to clarify the perspective from which this chapter has been written. Few previous attempts at understanding parental neglect have focused solely on the life situations of the mothers committing these acts. The goal of this chapter is to contextualize these actions so that we may gain a better understanding of how a mother so neglects the needs of her children that they die. Additionally, even fewer studies have examined the actions of these mothers from the perspective of privilege and power as they relate to disenfranchised groups within American society. Toward this end, a conceptualization of maternal filicide will be offered from the perspective of privilege and power, or lack thereof, the most striking elements linking all these cases together.

McIntosh,[1] in an essay discussing Euro-American ethnic and racial advantages, defines privilege as "an invisible package of unearned assets which I can count on cashing each day, but about which I was 'meant' to remain oblivious."[2] Moreover, she describes the term as an invisible weightless knapsack of special provisions, maps, passports, codebooks, visas, clothes, tools, and blank checks. In addition to ethnic and racial privilege, other features of unearned advantage include gender, heterosexuality, age, mental health, intelligence, physical ability, education, religion, nationality, and social and economic class.

A related construct that often accompanies discussions of privilege is the benefit from that privilege, often referred to as power. Depending on various schools of thought or historical traditions, scholars have defined power in many ways. In this brief introduction to power, two definitions will be presented. One scholar defines power as "the capacity to produce a change."[3] Accordingly, power can be differentiated more specifically in terms of the ability to increase one's own force, influence, or authority, as well as to control and limit that of others. Pinderhughes[4] defines power as one's capacity to influence the forces that affect one's life so that one may benefit from them. We might conceptualize powerlessness, then, as the inability to exercise such an influence. Perhaps we may begin to understand the apparently senseless reasons for maternal filicide through neglect through the lens of unearned advantages afforded by the constructs of privilege and power.

National Statistics

In 1998, the number of children victimized by child abuse and neglect in the United States was an estimated 903,000.[5] More than half of all reported cases, 53.5 percent, involved children who suffered solely from neglect, and an estimated 1,100 of these children died.[6] Undoubtedly, child neglect has been the most common type of reported and substantiated maltreatment of children throughout the last two decades. Individuals charged in these crimes were largely female, 60.4 percent, and the most common pattern of maltreatment, 44.7 percent, involved a child neglected by a female parent with no other persons identified.[7]

Why do mothers neglect their children at significantly higher rates than fathers? To understand why this discrepancy exists, it is essential to closely examine family structures within the United States. Between 1980 and 1999, the percentage of children living with one parent increased from 20 to 27 percent, and not surprisingly, 96 percent of children living with single parents live with a single mother.[8] Only 4 percent of children in the United States live with single fathers, a slight increase from 2 percent in 1980.[9] With such disproportionate numbers of children in the custody of their mothers rather than their fathers, it is easy to see why women rather than men are the ones usually charged with child neglect.

Defining Neglect-Omission

Before discussing additional demographic patterns, it is essential to clarify how the term "neglect" is defined within this typology. The 76 cases that formed the basis for this chapter involved mothers who did not purposely kill their children. Rather, the child's death was the result of two possible scenarios referred to as acts of omission or commission. In omission-based neglect, mothers failed to attend to the basic needs of their children, such as adequate nutrition or a safe environment with proper supervision. For example, consider the following case of neglect-omission that involved two mothers who left their children unattended in a locked apartment while they were gone for over twenty-four hours.

Chiquita Jackson and Tiffany McGee

From about 5:00 P.M. Monday to 3 A.M. Wednesday, Chiquita Jackson and Tiffany McGee of Miami, Florida, left their children unattended as they spent the evening driving around, having dinner, visiting with friends, and looking for shoplifting opportunities. The women left five of their young children, ages two to eight (one of whom had cerebral palsy) locked inside a bedroom without food, water, or access to a bathroom. Jackson secured the door by tying a strap from the boy's wheelchair around the doorknobs of the bedroom and the adjacent bathroom.

However, the children managed to get out of the bedroom and attempted to bathe their twenty-three-month-old sibling/cousin, but she drowned. Subsequently, the children were unable to turn off the water and flooded the apartment. The neighbor below noticed water leaking into his apartment and notified a maintenance worker. He knocked on the door, was let in by the children, and found the twenty-three-month-old toddler lying on the floor, already dead. Water had flooded both bathrooms and soaked the living room carpet in an apartment that was strewn with bits of food, soiled diapers, garbage, and feces. Both women were charged in the little girl's death.

In total, the Neglect-Omission subtype consisted of fifty-seven cases. Overall, the prevailing theme within neglect-omission cases was inadequate supervision.[10] As the cases were reviewed, six predominant methods emerged in the children's deaths.

Methods

Fire

In total, nine neglect cases involved filicide due in part to a lack of supervision by the mother when a fire broke out. In these cases, it was not uncommon for more than one child to die. Children were directly responsible for setting the fire in three cases (e.g., playing with matches) and three cases involved parents who were directly responsible for the fire (e.g., manufacturing methamphetamine in the home, a mother's smoldering cigarette, and attempting to thaw frozen water pipes). One case involved faulty attic wiring. In two of the cases, the cause of the fire could not be determined.

Automobile Suffocation

Three cases were grouped together because the circumstances around the deaths involved automobiles. They appeared to have the similar element of children who died from hyperthermia and/or suffocation after being locked inside a sweltering automobile. In two of those cases, the mothers had intentionally left the children strapped into their car seats while they visited with their boyfriends in motel rooms. In the other case, a mother's two children crawled into an unlocked car near the family's apartment and were unable to get out.[11]

Bathtub Drowning

Twelve cases involved children who drowned as a result of being inadequately supervised while in the bathtub. These cases often involved mothers who stepped out of the bathroom to perform another task such as answering the telephone or attending to the needs of another child, and consequently inadequately supervising the bathing child. Slightly different circumstances contributed to the child's death in another case. A nine-year-old and his infant sibling were left unattended when their mother's child care arrangements fell through. When the older child attempted to bathe the younger one, the baby drowned, and the mother was charged.

Layover Suffocation

Eight cases involved children who suffocated. In six cases, the children were suffocated as the mother, who was nursing the child either in bed or on the sofa, fell asleep and rolled over onto the child. One case concerned an infant who was suffocated by blankets as she and her five other siblings slept in the bed they shared with their mother. The last case involved a mother who, in an attempt to stop her child from crying by creating a dark space, placed her child in a car seat and put the car seat in a closet. The child rolled out of the car seat and onto a pile of clothes where she suffocated.

Nutrition

Fifteen cases in this cluster had a similar pattern involving mothers who failed to maintain the nutritional needs of the child. These actions resulted in the child's death through dehydration and/or starvation.

Inattention to Safety Needs

Ten cases involved mothers who inadequately attended to the safety needs of their children, thereby bringing about the child's death. For example, one mother left cigarette butts on the coffee table which her daughter subsequently ingested and which caused her to choke to death.

Defining Neglect-Commission

The second type of neglect is referred to as commission-based neglect. In this type of death, mothers were irresponsible in their reaction to a child's behavior and their actions brought about the death of the child. Consistent with women placed in neglect-omission, mothers in this category did not purposely kill their children, but filicide occurred nonetheless. All these cases involved the mother's attempt to stop the child's crying. Although several deaths were initially considered to be cases of sudden infant death syndrome, it was later determined that asphyxiation had occurred. Consider the following case of a mother who placed toilet tissue in her infant daughter's mouth to stop her cries.

Deniece Helms

Deniece Helms, twenty years old, tried for three hours to quiet the cries of her nine-month-old daughter. After changing the baby's diapers, holding and feeding the baby, her cries would not cease. Helms told investigators that she held toilet tissue in the baby's mouth, even though the baby struggled to spit it out. Helms went to bed after the incident and called police the following morning. On previous occasions, she admitted to placing a sock in the child's throat to quiet her, but indicated that her daughter was always able to spit it out. Helms pled guilty to second-degree murder and faces up to twenty-five years in prison.

In total, the Neglect-Commission subtype was made up of nineteen cases. As the cases were reviewed, two predominant methods emerged in the children's deaths.

Methods

Direct

In eleven cases the child's death resulted from shaking the baby, slamming the baby's head into the side of the bed, throwing the child across the room, or hurling the baby out the window.

Indirect

In eight cases the baby died as the result of suffocation when the mother placed something over the child's head, such as a pillow or plastic bag. In one case, the mother stuffed a baby wipe into the child's mouth in an effort to muffle the baby's crying, and in another case toilet tissue was used.

The first reaction to the acts described above is usually that of disbelief and outrage. Typically, the next reaction is one of condemnation of the mother as we contemplate what might have led her to commit such unbelievable acts. This chapter will explore the life situations of mothers who killed their children through acts of neglect. The initial section of this chapter will delineate characteristics that mothers in this category share. Factors that will be addressed include maternal age, marital status, socioeconomic status, family size, social support systems, parenting knowledge, mental health issues such as maternal depression and substance abuse, and ethnocultural considerations. The final section of this chapter will focus on addressing the implications for intervention brought about by this examination of cases.

A Profile of Mothers Who Kill Their Children through Neglectful Acts

In general, the mothers in this category are young, single, have large families, are lacking in social support systems, and are of lower socioeconomic status. Moreover, they have received fewer years of formal education, may suffer from depression, and may possibly use alcohol or other drugs. Clearly, the women represented in this category enjoy few, if any, elements of privilege and the consequent power to affect change. As a profile of mothers who kill their children through neglectful acts is established, each characteristic will be delineated within the context of the mothers' collective societal disempowerment and exceedingly limited number of unearned advantages and opportunities. Through this careful analysis, the underpinnings of how seemingly loving and caring mothers kill their children through neglect will be revealed.

Maternal Age

Jennie Bain Ducker

In 1995, Jennie Bain Ducker, twenty-one, of McMinnville, Tennessee, left her two sons, twenty-three months and twelve months, in the car while she spent the evening in her boyfriend's motel room. Before leaving the boys, Ducker strapped them in their car seats, propped up bottles from which to drink, and locked the doors of the car, which had tinted windows. Periodically throughout the evening Ducker peered down on the children from the second-story balcony as she "partied" in the motel room. Ducker claimed she fell asleep at 5:00 A.M. and woke up at noon. Investigators estimated that her blood alcohol content was two times the legal limit for drivers when she fell asleep.

The children had been strapped in the car seats for approximately eight to ten hours and as the sun came up, the temperature inside the car increased to an estimated 120 degrees. When the children were brought to the hospital they were dead on arrival. Ducker was soon charged with first-degree murder and was ultimately convicted of aggravated child abuse. She was sentenced to eighteen years in prison with eligibility for parole in six years.

The average age of mothers at the time the filicide occurred was 25.51 years. When separated into omission and commission-based neglect, the average age of mothers was 26.38 years and 23.21 years, respectively. Most mothers were twenty years old when their child(ren) died. The average age when the women in this category became mothers was 22.51 years, and the majority became mothers between the ages of 17 and 20.

Jennie Bain Ducker was clearly unable to give the needs of her children equal or greater priority than her own perceived needs. Despite her efforts to ensure their safety by locking them in the car, checking on them throughout the night by peering down from the motel balcony, and making sure they could access their bottles, this young mother lacked the psychological maturity to recognize that in fact her children were in an incredibly unsafe situation. Many young mothers are unable to make such distinctions, and often their poor judgment in parenting decisions leads to fatality.

After reviewing the cases in this category, it became clear that the majority of mothers had not yet formed or were in the process of forming their own identity when they became parents. Most of these women went straight from the developmental stage of adolescence to parenting with little, if any, time to establish a solid sense of self. The demands of parenting were so great for this group of mothers that after their children were born, they had limited opportunity to continue to grow personally. Consequently, young mothers may be more vulnerable to pressures to take part in the activities of the developmental stage from which they were abruptly removed, such as partying with friends in a motel room. Many of the cases involved a parent's pursuit of personal interests over responsible parenting behaviors. It is important to point out that young fathers typically do not face such conflicting desires as they rarely serve as the primary caretakers of their children. Consider another example:

Tami Lynn Richards

In January 1998, Tami Lynn Richards, twenty-four, of Colorado, left her two children, three years old and eighteen months, unsupervised in their apartment as she spent three hours socializing. Initially, Richards told police she had stepped out of her apartment briefly to check her mail and walk around her apartment complex to reflect on her pending divorce. She later admitted leaving the apartment to drink at a local bar and to hear a band play.

Before Richards left she placed two safety gates on the bedroom door to keep her children inside. However, her three-year-old son got out of the room and set a pile of clothes on fire while playing with matches. Neighbors heard the smoke alarm and attempted to rescue the children with little success. After police arrived, the children were taken to a nearby hospital and pronounced dead. Richards was convicted of two counts of child abuse resulting in death and sentenced to thirty-two years in prison.

A young mother's lack of maturity may have other far-reaching implications. First, she may be viewed differently by her peer network simply because of her role as a parent, which may lead to feelings of isolation from previous social connections. Moreover, she may feel alienated from more mature mothers who may have some of the privileges she lacks, including a partner with whom to share parenting responsibilities and financial resources. Her young age may make her less aware of community resources, such as educational programs for new mothers and infants, as those programs may not be marketed to women in her age group. Young mothers may also be less sophisticated in navigating large beauracratic systems such as public assistance programs and may not even be aware that they exist. Lastly, there may be fewer opportunities for mentoring by more experienced mothers because they may perceive their young age as an embarrassment and may be less inclined to reach out for help.

Marital Status

An overwhelming majority of mothers in this category, approximately 85 percent, were single parents. Many similar themes in the life situations of single mothers emerged and easily divided into two primary domains: lack of financial and emotional resources. In terms of financial resources, women earn significantly less than men throughout the world regardless of marital status. Certainly, the effects of this wage discrepancy become even more pronounced when the woman is the sole provider for the family. The role that limited income played in the lives of these women will be elaborated upon as the characteristic of poverty is discussed later in this analysis.

The emotional resources of the mothers serving as single parents are severely depleted in this category. Hence it is not surprising that when only one parent is present to handle the demands of child rearing, the stresses placed on that individual abound. The majority of these women had very little personal time, which had many implications for the way they responded to stressful situations. For many of the mothers in the neglect-commission subcategory, there was little time to gain a perspective on their particular parenting situations. For instance, if a mother who responded to an incessantly crying child by impulsively shaking the baby to death, had had more personal time, one might speculate that she may have had more psychological resources available to her and may have had better judgment in the situation. Moreover, she may have had greater opportunities to discuss alternative courses of action with friends and family. Another reality for these mothers included limited contact with other adults because they spent nearly all their time attending to both parenting and household duties. In more practical terms, this meant that there were fewer individuals with whom they could collaborate about parenting strategies and process the experiences of single motherhood.

The emotional resources of single mothers were further depleted because, in addition to providing all the child care, they also had to run the entire household. They had to clean the house, wash the clothes, prepare the meals, pay the bills, and make needed household repairs. With so many demands placed upon them, their emotional resources were thoroughly overtaxed.

Lastly, when a partner was residing in the home, marital or relationship stress was often occurring around the time of the filicide. Of the 15 percent of cases in which there was a partner in the home, 54 percent involved mothers who were in the process of separating or divorcing near the time of the neglectful behavior. Additionally, arguments with boyfriends or partners, which frequently resulted in domestic violence, occurred in 11 percent of all cases reviewed. The following is a case example of a mother who smothered her infant daughter after an instance of domestic violence.

Diana Lynn Hesse

Diana Lynn Hesse, nineteen, of Tampa, Florida, smothered her six-week-old daughter with a pillow to stop the child from crying. Hesse told officials that she was cleaning her house for a visit by state social workers when she became so overwhelmed by the child's cries that she placed a pillow in her daughter's crib. Between midnight and 8:00 A.M., Hesse smothered her baby. On September 29, the same day she killed her daughter, the child's father was arrested and charged with aggravated battery for beating Hesse. Reports also indicated that Hesse came from a "busted" home.

Hesse was originally arrested on a first-degree murder charge. However, prosecutors later reduced the indictment to second-degree murder. The difference in charges within the state of Florida is that Hesse, if convicted, would not face life in prison. As part of a plea agreement, Hesse pled guilty to manslaughter and was sentenced to fifteen years in prison, to be suspended after five and a half years.

This case is representative of a mother who was clearly struggling with her own traumatic experiences. As a result, she may have lacked the psychological resources necessary to respond appropriately to her crying child.

Poverty

Etirza Eversley

Etirza Eversley, a twenty-two-year-old single mother, arranged for her newborn infant to be cared for by another woman because she had neither the psychological nor financial resources to care for him. However, two months later, Eversley decided to bring the child home to her duplex apartment where she was raising her two other children, ages two and four. Noticing the baby had a cough, she took her son to a public health clinic, and physicians at the clinic instructed this young mother to take the baby to the emergency room. When Eversley arrived at the ER she noticed three people ahead of her in line and chose not to wait. The next morning the baby died of pneumonia. Eversley was convicted of manslaughter and was to receive nine to fifteen years in prison, but her charge was dropped to misdemeanor child abuse and she received the maximum sentence of 364 days in jail.

This case describes a woman who was about to be evicted from her apartment because of limited financial resources. Similar economic circumstances prevailed in approximately 90 percent of the cases in this category which involved women and children living in poverty. As mentioned, the effects of wage discrepancies between men and women become even more prominent when women are the sole breadwinners in a family. Limited earning potential for women amounts to decreased societal power and fewer privileges in numerous ways. It was common for mothers in this category to use public assistance, a stressful system to navigate, to augment their meager salaries in order to provide for their children's most basic needs, such as food, housing, and clothing. Other basic needs which the mothers were unable to meet on their limited income included funds to pay for exterminators to come in when bugs and rodents permeated the home or for babysitters to provide a much needed respite. Moreover, mothers in this category could rarely afford medical care to treat their sick children, and although Medicaid offers coverage, it also offers a different set of challenges. For instance, the availability of providers is severely limited as many physicians choose not to see patients with Medicaid. Furthermore, Medicaid patients often only receive treatment on a specific day of the week in a particular office which may be several towns away.

Family Size

Another factor, which only compounds the issue of limited financial resources for women and children in this category, is the number of family members who must be supported by the mother's income to meet their needs. Simply put, a greater number of children in the family leads to fewer privileges for all the members. Among the cases reviewed, 41 percent involved families with three or more children. Consider the next case.

Christina Amaker

Christina Amaker, twenty-eight, of Columbus, Ohio, was indicted in the suffocation death of her thirteen-day-old daughter. The infant was sleeping in a crowded twin bed occupied by Amaker and at least five of her six other children, ranging in ages from one through ten. The infant was found the next morning underneath her three-year-old brother and a pile of blankets.

Amaker testified that she moved from Pittsburgh to Columbus in late 1995 after she and her kids were evicted from a home that they shared with Amaker's mother. She stated that she had struggled to find housing for such a large family and spent a month in a homeless shelter when housing plans fell through. Amaker, who had no prior court record, was charged with involuntary manslaughter and child endangering. Although acquitted of all charges, she was unable to get her children back until she found suitable housing.

Many studies illustrate that neglectful families tend to be larger, with more children in the home than non-neglecting counterparts.[12] In practical terms, more children in the family means there are more mouths to feed, dishes to wash, clothes to buy, teeth to brush, visits to health facilities when the kids are sick, teachers to confer with when problems arise at school, and on and on. All these familial responsibilities take away from the mother's ability to replenish her depleted psychological energy, and as indicated previously, this may affect her judgment. For example, one might speculate that from Christine Amaker's perspective, she was meeting her children's needs by providing a warm bed in which to sleep. But she may not have had the mental energy to recognize the potential consequences of such a sleeping arrangement. Moreover, even if she had been able to foresee the dangers, it is unlikely she would have the power to fix the situation by purchasing beds for each member of the family.

Social Support Systems

Given the data we had available for review, it was a challenge to attempt to quantify a neglectful mother's perceived and received social support. But in general, we found that feelings of isolation from peers and disenfranchisement from society were consistent themes in the group. Across all the cases, it became evident that mothers at greatest risk for neglect also felt unsupported by both their nuclear and extended family systems.

Bishop and Leadbeater have examined the relationship between maternal social support and child maltreatment.[13] They found that, despite a similar number of persons in the social networks of maltreating mothers and controls, maltreating mothers did not feel that their networks were providing adequate support. In addition, maltreating mothers reported decreased contact with friends and rated the quality of support from friends as lower than that of nonmaltreating mothers.[14]

Many hypotheses exist to explain why neglectful mothers have decreased support systems and perceive the quality of support from friends and family as poor. First and foremost, one might presume that disenfranchised mothers do in fact require more support than mothers who enjoy the benefits of privilege. Alternatively, maltreating mothers may seek to avoid contact outside their families as a way of preventing others from detecting their unsatisfactory parenting skills,[15] thereby contributing to increased feelings of isolation. Conversely, these mothers may simply choose not to access systems that they feel have failed them in the past, perhaps because these systems have proved to be incompetent supports time and again. Research also indicates that neglectful mothers may have social networks dominated by critical, rather than supportive, friends and relatives.[16] Or, on the other hand, they may perceive themselves to be bad mothers. For instance, they likely internalize the disapproving looks they receive from more privileged individuals in society who pass judgment on them when they are unable to access healthcare for their sick children or are unable to purchase their children winter hats, an unaffordable luxury.

Knowledge

Our data rarely allowed us to determine the knowledge base from which a mother made her parenting decisions. However, we divided this construct into two domains—formal academic education and effective parenting skills education—and made inferences accordingly.

Given the limited financial resources of the mothers in this category, one might speculate that the number of years they spent in formal academic settings was minimal. In general, maltreating parents have less formal education than nonmaltreating parents. One study revealed that neglectful mothers were less likely to have completed high school. At the beginning of the study, only 11 percent had completed high school compared with 32 percent of non-neglecting mothers.[17] In 1998, the overall high school completion rates for young adults ages 18 to 24 was 85 percent, a small decline from the 86 percent in 1997.[18]

Mothers with limited education may be less inclined or lack the capacity to seek out reading materials to help them parent. In practical terms, they may have less knowledge about effective parenting strategies and/or knowledge of child development on subjects ranging from how to appropriately secure a child's car seat in place to how to effectively respond to a crying infant. These mothers also lack the financial resources necessary to readily purchase books, audiocassettes, videos, and the like, or attend seminars to help them acquire the skills necessary to make their parenting interventions more effective. Presumably, if they do happen to have extra money, they likely have more immediate needs.

Mental Health

Attempting to understand a mother's previous mental health history was one of our goals when we reviewed the data. In 41 percent of the cases, mothers were experiencing some form of psychological problem. Overall, two main types of mental health issues prevailed: mood disorders and chemical dependency.

Mood Disorders

We suspect that rates of depression among this group of women are relatively high. Although only six cases specifically noted a psychological disorder such as Major Depression, it is likely that mood disorders are actually much greater than indicated by the newspaper articles. We assume this to be so because rates of depression among women are nearly twice as high as among men[19] and this disorder often goes undiagnosed unless formal mental health treatment is sought. Clearly, with limited time and resources, such treatment was probably not a high priority for the women.

It became apparent that many of the mothers were experiencing feelings of low self-esteem. This construct, often comorbid with depression, has been implicated as a risk factor in the etiology of child maltreatment.[20] Major depression was a significant contributing factor in the following case:

Jennifer Mayer

Jennifer Mayer, twenty-one, from El Cajon, California, had suffered from depression throughout her life according to court records. In fact, Mayer had been hospitalized twice during her teenage years when her bouts of depression had become especially severe. So when her son died in his bedroom of severe chronic malnutrition, Mayer's attorney contended that she was in the midst of profound psychological depression. It was argued that her poor mental health caused her to be unaware of her son's malnutrition, and unable to fully recognize her son's distress.

Her son weighed only nineteen pounds at the time of his death, twelve pounds less than the expected weight for a three-year-old child. His body had very little muscle or body fat, and in a final effort to stay alive, his body had begun to consume itself. Another sign of neglect was that his genital area was covered with sores from untreated diaper rash.

Mayer was convicted of second-degree murder and was sentenced to fifteen years to life in prison. David Mayer was also implicated in his son's death as it was argued that he was primarily responsible for the child's care while his wife worked as a full-time cook. He was convicted of first-degree murder, receiving twenty-five years to life in prison. He told authorities that "God did not like fat babies."[21]

In general, the stresses of parenting young children will probably result in fatigue or decreased energy among the parents. Likewise, with such limited power and privilege, it is easy to see why feelings of sadness, excessive guilt, low self-esteem, isolation, and worthlessness may frequently arise among these mothers. Furthermore, it is easy to understand why mothers living in poverty, who are aware that their chances of improving or changing their life situations are limited due to their limited education, young age, sole parenting responsibility, and ultimately societal gender bias, experience depression. Certainly, if they perceive their life experiences to be unchanging, they may feel hopeless to change their life situation.

Chemical Dependency

There was substance use and abuse in 34 percent of the cases. The use of illicit substances has been strongly implicated in the occurrence of child neglect.[22] In fact, of the psychiatric disorders that have been studied, substance abuse disorders appear to be the most commonly associated with the maltreatment of children.[23] Obviously, when mothers abuse substances the potential for harm to their children significantly increases, as demonstrated in the following case.

Karen Henderson

Karen Henderson, twenty-one, of Bakersfield, California, began taking drugs when she was fifteen, not long after she had been raped by her mother's boyfriend. Tragically, her two-month old son, whom she was breastfeeding, died after drinking breast milk that was laced with the drug. Her defense attorney argued that she took the drug because she reported that she became so worried that she might fall asleep and be unable to care for her baby and two other children, and that there was no one to assist her with seemingly endless responsibilities.

Henderson, who was using public assistance to provide for her family, had a history of substance abuse. Social workers warned her not to breastfeed her baby if she used drugs. With the pressures and demands of single parenting exhausting her daily, Henderson stated that she used "crank," a cheap addictive methamphetamine, to stay awake so that she could watch her children. She was found guilty of child endangerment and sentenced to six years in prison.

Not only can a mother's substance abuse directly impact a child, as reflected in the case above, but there are also more indirect effects that are just as damaging. For instance, a mother's poor financial situation is only exacerbated when she is using some of her income to buy alcohol or drugs. This takes away money needed to buy food, purchase clothes, and pay for medical care. Additionally, the mother's psychological resources to parent effectively or be mindful of the safety needs of her children are severely compromised.

Ethnocultural/Classist Considerations

Shawntello Young

Shawntello Young lived with ten other family members in their five-bedroom Atlanta Housing Authority apartment. Her eight-month-old daughter suffocated to death after choking on a cockroach that became lodged in her throat, blocking her airway. The Young family and other residents reported a long-standing roach, ant, and rat infestation problem at the forty-year-old public housing complex. They said the infestation began about four years prior to the child's death, and on one occasion they found two snakes inside their apartment. Shortly after the infant died, a Housing Department Inspector went to the home in which he found dead roaches in the apartment and witnessed a rat run out of a hole in the kitchen.

Young discussed the chronic nature of these problems as she recalled an experience with her first child. "The cockroaches were crawling all over her in the crib. I took that bed out {of} there that day and just let her sleep with me."[24]

Although no criminal charges were filed against Young, social service investigators went to the home the day of the infant's death to assess the case for child abuse and neglect. Agents quickly learned that the child had been well cared for. One must consider whether or not an upper-middle-class woman residing in the suburbs would have been subjected to the same treatment. In an editorial written in response to actions taken by the Fulton County Department of Family and Children Services, friends of the Young family wrote, "In suburbia, the finger-pointing in a tragedy like this is settled discretely. In the projects, the mother is grilled by the police and the dead child examined for signs of abuse or neglect. Most white suburban children achieve their success as the product of generations of ready access to the privileges and rewards of American society. Most African-American families are starting from ground zero in this generation."[25]

Issues of ethnic and racial background and class are often intertwined by society. Clearly, underscoring almost every case in this category is the issue of low economic status and the resulting discrimination directed at families living in poverty. But issues distinct to either class or race become intermingled as persons of color are overrepresented in the lower socioeconomic strata. For instance, 57 percent of black children will experience at least one year of life below the poverty line in comparison to 15 percent of white children.[26] Subsequently, these families are more vulnerable to the reporting and substantiation of child maltreatment due to the combined effects of blatant racism, poverty, ethnocultural stereotypes, and the culturally sanctioned use of physical discipline.[27] It is not surprising, then, that these mothers and children experience numerous injustices within the child welfare system, such as higher reports of child maltreatment[28] than their white counterparts.

Intervention: Full-Service Pediatric Community Healthcare Center

As demonstrated in the preceding analysis, mothers who commit fatal child neglect are in need of extensive assistance in numerous areas, both global and specific. This final section of the chapter will focus on one intervention that could significantly decrease the risk of fatal child neglect, namely, the establishment of multidisciplinary full-service pediatric healthcare centers.

It is imperative that professionals provide a continuum of care for neglectful mothers. One way to accomplish this is by establishing comprehensive pediatric health centers, specifically targeting the zero to three population, as most neglected children fall within this age range. Typically neglectful mothers must travel from agency to agency and town to town as they seek services such as public assistance benefits, prenatal care, medical and dental care, mental health intervention, and parenting skills training. The creation of full-service pediatric community healthcare centers would allow for a facility where the needs of both parents and children can be fulfilled. Support for such a model has already been seen in one innovative program called Healthy Steps.[29]

The Healthy Steps for Young Children Program, funded in collaboration with community-based foundations, local healthcare providers, and the Commonwealth Fund, is dedicated to healthcare delivery to children during the first three years of life. Toward this end, close partnerships are created between mothers and healthcare professionals to address not only the physical needs of the child, but also emotional and intellectual growth as well as healthy child development. In addition to physicians and nurses, the model utilizes Healthy Steps Specialists[30] who have specific training in child development and who focus their services on behavioral and developmental issues for children. The Specialists have many roles within the program, including conducting home visits to support and enhance interactions between the parent and infant, conducting ongoing checkups that assess both child development and family factors, helping mothers manage common behavioral concerns such as fussiness, sleep, or discipline problems, facilitating parent education groups, and staffing a telephone information line to answer questions about child development. Essentially, the Healthy Steps holistic approach views the promotion of children's development and assistance to parents as primary goals when treating a child's physical illnesses. Since its inception in 1994, the Health Steps program has grown steadily and has developed partnerships with numerous pediatric and family practice sites across the United States.

To effectively establish such a full-service pediatric healthcare center, it is crucial to establish grassroots involvement and academic-community partnerships. Grassroots involvement or support by members of the community is essential because the problem of child neglect is not an individual one, but one that the entire community must address. In an effort to assess and increase community interest in the project by holding community meetings and planning sessions, local funding sources should be called upon to make financial contributions. Area hospitals, for instance, would have a vested interest in the center's success because such a facility would benefit the hospital by providing a continuity of care for underserved populations when individuals are discharged. Donations by local residents and other forms of grassroots involvement would also help ensure the center's success, as a sense of ownership in the facility by the community would be engendered.

Another step in successfully creating such a full-service health center is establishing academic-community partnerships. The reasons for such partnerships are limitless, but most importantly, linking universities to community initiatives allows for the creation of service learning experiences. For example, medical and nursing students could provide care in the center, which would not only enhance their academic training, but also allow for service delivery to underserved populations. Similarly, students in the field of dentistry and optometry could provide dental and eye care. Psychology students could provide developmental assessment and deliver psychotherapy services. Students in the field of social work could assist families in applying for public assistance programs or national health insurance programs, provide education in the area of parent skills training, or deliver additional mental health services. Finally, law students could provide mothers with legal counseling or family advocacy services. Ultimately, through such a model everyone wins. Patients receive much needed services, students obtain experiential training in their respective fields and also gain experience working with disenfranchised groups of society, thereby becoming more likely to practice in similar communities when they are professionals. Universities are also able to fulfill part of their mission, which often involves service to the community. Most importantly, the community is greatly able to increase the well-being of children and at the same time decrease the risk for neglect by supporting and educating parents.

Certainly, the initiatives that could be pursued by such a facility are infinite, but a key feature to each center is the incorporation of parent education into every single visit. The next section addresses the various types of programming that could be offered through health centers espousing a full-service model.

Psychoeducational Groups

Psychoeducational groups for mothers experiencing stress would be key, and the goals of such groups would be twofold. Not only would parenting skills and child development be taught, but the emotional development surrounding motherhood would also be addressed. Mothers would be educated on the expectations they should have for themselves in their new role as parents and how their emotions and feelings will likely change and evolve as their children grow.

One such topic, for example, might involve the issue of crying babies. Mothers in the group would be informed that babies cry extensively when they are newborns, and that this crying can often be very frustrating, so much so that they may experience a desire to suffocate or shake their baby. Rather than condemning mothers for such ideas, these thoughts would be validated and normalized by the group facilitator and probably by other mothers in the group. Appropriately, education on effective ways of handling such stressful situations would then be provided.

Mentoring Programs

Mentoring programs for young mothers with limited resources would be beneficial interventions. In such a program, any mother identified as being at risk for neglecting her children would have the option of being paired off with a more experienced volunteer mother. These types of pairings could provide struggling mothers with a personal resource for discussing parenting concerns, but more importantly, would provide that mother with individual attention and companionship during stressful times. Such interactions can help decrease the mother's sense of social disconnectedness.

The benefits of such programs are far-reaching and, in addition to decreasing the sense of isolation, these initiatives would enhance a mother's perceived connectedness with the outside world, increase her social connections with other adults, and validate the difficulties and stresses of parenting. Furthermore, child care would be provided during all group interventions, which would increase a mother's personal time by providing a respite from her children.

Anger Management Training

It has been clearly demonstrated in this chapter that mothers who neglect their children have significantly limited psychological energy with which to handle the stresses of parenting, and consequently become irritated and frustrated much more quickly than mothers who have such energy. Therefore it is essential to provide these mothers with anger management skills. The topics that need to be addressed include identifying anger triggers and physiological responses to anger, impulse control training, and ways to enhance low frustration tolerance. Mastery of these skills will help increase the mother's awareness of whether she should intervene with her child after she assesses her level of anger or frustration.

Once a mother has accurately identified her anger responses, it is essential to provide her with effective coping resources. Mothers should learn skills like "time out" during which they remove themselves from stressful situations. This may entail leaving the child and briefly taking a moment to gain perspective on a situation. Or professionals may teach them more direct relaxation training skills such as progressive muscle relaxation, deep breathing, and visualization.

Parent-Skills Education

At each visit to one of the service providers listed above, mothers should receive a pamphlet or be able to check out videos related to caring for their children. As mentioned above, the information provided should focus not solely on safety awareness and parenting skills, but also on self-care information for overwhelmed parents. The safety topics addressed in these handouts should include nutritional needs, car suffocation, bathtub drowning, appropriate sleeping precautions, and fire safety.

Finally, there is every reason to continue the movement toward comprehensive full-service pediatric healthcare centers. Once committed healthcare providers are identified, residents in the community offer support, funders invest in the vision and mission, and academic partnerships are established, the problems of inadequate service delivery to mothers and children can be challenged and the problems of neglect can be addressed.

Conclusion

Outrage and contempt for women who neglect their children are typical reactions as each of us struggles to understand a mother who neglects her children so severely that death results. However, as the characteristics of such cases are revealed and clarified, these filicides become less shocking and people want to support, rather than condemn, the mothers concerned.

As we analyze the complex life experiences of these women from the perspective of privilege and power, it becomes quite clear why these crimes occur and why it is easier to perceive that it is "them" and not "us" who could unintentionally kill their children. Those of us privileged by virtue of age, wealth, education, solid support systems, and the collective emotional well-being that results from these benefits must be catalysts in helping mothers who find themselves isolated, disempowered, and above all disenfranchised from society.

Perhaps most importantly, we must reach out to these women as they will probably not reach out to us for the assistance and support they so desperately need. It is incumbent upon all women to create a safe haven where the difficult realities of motherhood can be discussed. It is at this starting point that we may begin to help mothers who neglect their children. In the words of Jean Baker Miller, "once we recognize the undeniable truth that the world has been explained so far without the close observation of women's experience, it is easier to consider that seemingly 'unreal' possibilities can become real."[31]

5

ABUSE-RELATED DEATHS

❏

Awilda Lopez was born in Puerto Rico, one of thirteen children. Awilda grew up in New York's inner city. In grade school she received honor certificates and good attendance awards. However, when Awilda became an adolescent, she began dating, got pregnant, married the father of her baby, and dropped out of school. In 1988, she tried crack cocaine, to which she quickly became addicted, and started a downward spiral. With no money to pay the rent, the family, now with two children, was forced to leave their apartment. Awilda and her husband split up and she lived in homeless shelters. During one of those stays, Awilda had a brief relationship with Gustavo Izquierdo, an employee of the shelter and a Cuban immigrant. Awilda became pregnant and bore a crack-addicted child named Elisa Izquierdo. Awilda had already lost custody of her two children and when Elisa was born lost custody of her as well. In order to regain custody, Awilda would have to stay off drugs and attend parenting classes. Elisa went to live with her father.

During the next year, Awilda outwardly appeared to piece her life together and regained custody of her two older children. Part of her rehabilitation seemed to be her new marriage to Carlos Lopez. Unfortunately, Carlos was an alcoholic who had violent tendencies. In 1991, Carlos accused Awilda of seeing other men and stabbed her seventeen times with a pocketknife. When Carlos returned from jail, he allegedly began directing most of his violence toward his stepchildren. More neglect allegations were reported and Awilda tested positive for cocaine use. Awilda was also hospitalized after a suicide attempt in 1994. She was later dismissed from a drug program due to poor attendance and inappropriate behavior. When the family moved from one area of New York City to another in April 1994, their file was not transferred. In fact, as of December 1995, it still could not be located. By this time, Awilda had three more children.

Meanwhile, Elisa was flourishing. Gustavo wanted only the best for her. He took parenting classes and enrolled her in a Montessori program, despite the fact he really could not afford it. Miraculously, fate stepped in. Prince Michael of Greece saw Elisa at school, grew fond of the child, and offered to pay for her private schooling through high school. She was described as beautiful and radiant. Still, Elisa indicated her mother hit and hurt her during visits and there were bruises on her body and injuries to her vaginal area. School officials noticed adjustment issues arise after Elisa visited her mother and reported Awilda to a child abuse hotline. Gustavo requested Elisa's visits with her mother be supervised but his request was never granted. Then, unfortunately, Gustavo died of lung cancer in May 1994. Gustavo's cousin petitioned for custody of Elisa but so did Awilda. The Montessori director wrote the judge in the custody hearing and indicated she thought the cousin should be awarded custody because of Awilda's history of drug and child abuse. Elisa's new caseworker, who had never visited the cousin's home, and had only visited Awilda's once, testified for Awilda. So did Elisa's court-appointed guardian and a caseworker from a nonprofit agency called Project Chance. Awilda was granted custody and quickly pulled Elisa out of the Montessori program.

In September 1994, Elisa began kindergarten at a public school. School officials began reporting suspected child abuse. They noticed Elisa walked with a limp, urinated frequently, her hair was thinning and she had a rash on her scalp. By early 1995, Elisa was no longer in attendance at school. In February, Project Chance wrote the child protection manager indicating that Elisa was being neglected. On March 14, an anonymous letter arrived at the child welfare office indicating Awilda had cut off all Elisa's hair and confined her for long periods in a dark room. On March 20, Elisa was admitted to the hospital with a fractured shoulder, which had been left untreated for three days. She was not examined for previous fractures but the physician reported his child abuse suspicions. Elisa missed follow-up visits but no one investigated. In April, caseworkers from Project Chance suggested Awilda hospitalize Elisa in a psychiatric hospital. They had noted that Elisa was withdrawn, smearing her feces on the refrigerator, setting fires, suffering from delusions and hallucinations, and burying her urine-soaked underwear in a hole under the bed. In addition, Awilda was distraught. Awilda agreed to hospitalize Elisa but changed her mind during the six-hour wait in the emergency room. She was referred for outpatient counseling, but again there was no follow-up after one appointment. The hospital did not notify child welfare. Awilda stopped returning calls from Project Chance. In September, Awilda told school officials Elisa had transferred to another school but they never verified this information.

On November 22, 1995, Elisa was found dead. Awilda had hit Elisa so hard that she slammed against a concrete wall, hitting her head. For two days Elisa lay unresponsive in bed and fluid leaked from her mouth. Finally, she died. The coroner detailed the extent of the abuse Elisa had suffered. It included physical abuses such as broken fingers, bruises, and cigarette burns. However, it became quickly apparent that Elisa had suffered other abuses. She had been repeatedly raped and sodomized, sometimes with a hairbrush. Later, her mother revealed that Elisa was forced to eat her own feces and drink ammonia. On at least one occasion, Awilda mopped the floor with Elisa's head and hair. In defending some of her actions, Awilda indicated that Elisa's dead father had practiced Santeria and his relatives had forced Elisa to eat snakes and satanic potions, which in turn caused her to be possessed by the devil. Awilda said she had attempted to remove the snakes and potions by squeezing Elisa's stomach and inserting a hairbrush in the girl's rectum. During these episodes Awilda indicated she would turn the stereo up loud so neighbors would not hear Elisa's screams. Awilda also maintained that some of Elisa's injuries were self-inflicted. In one reported statement, Awilda claimed Elisa was so strong, because she was possessed, that she could lift heavy objects, which fell and broke her finger and toe.

In April 1996, one psychologist was fired and another suspended for altering records related to Elisa. In June, Awilda Lopez agreed to plead guilty to second-degree murder to spare her children a trial. She was sentenced to fifteen years to life. Her attorney said Awilda "wanted to be able to maybe get out of jail at a somewhat early age to reassume a family life."[1] In September, Elisa's caseworker was dismissed for not making required home visits and not properly investigating allegations of abuse. His supervisor was also later terminated. In October 1996, Carlos Lopez pled guilty to attempted assault in the second degree and received a maximum sentence of three years. He indicated he was innocent of the charges but wanted to spare making his children testify.

Research Related to Mothers Who Batter Their Children

Women who abuse their children have received scant research attention. In part, this may be due to definitional issues. For example, a fine line often distinguishes abuse from neglect. In addition, there are clear ethnic and cultural variations regarding what constitutes acceptable disciplinary practices and what is abusive. Although no one has offered a clear definition of abuse, everyone seems to "know it when they see it." Generally only extreme cases, such as that of Awilda Lopez, come to public attention.

Instead of creating a profile of abusive mothers, researchers have chosen to theorize and examine risk factors that may be related to maternal abuse. Clearly the factor that has received the most attention, as it relates to both parents, is the Intergenerational Transmission Hypothesis.[2] Quite simply, this theory suggests that abuse as a child or observation of abuse of a child, is related to abuse as a parent. Another approach is the transactional model.[3] In this model prior abuse may predispose someone to abuse but its actual occurrence depends on a host of mitigating and aggravating circumstances. For example, although it is unclear whether Awilda Lopez was abused, her mother was once beaten so severely while she was pregnant that the child was born paralyzed. However, despite exposure to numerous aggravating circumstances such as being a teenage mother and living in poverty, Awilda Lopez did not appear to abuse her children and was not reported to be involved with child welfare until after she began using drugs, another aggravating factor.

In addition to poverty, adolescent parenting, and drug use, lack of emotional support, poor social skills, domestic violence, and depression have been suggested as possible aggravating factors for maternal child abuse. Recent research has provided further confirmation for the increased abuse potential of adolescent mothers in general, but particularly impoverished mothers. Lee and George[4] found that when they controlled other sociodemographic variables, maternal age and poverty were strong predictors of child maltreatment. In another study, researchers tracked a group of pregnant adolescent women and a group of adult pregnant women for approximately a year and a half postpartum.[5] The women had been matched on other sociodemographic variables at the start of the research. Adolescent mothers had higher abuse potential and depression scores than adult mothers.

In general, depressed mothers have more thoughts of harming their child than do nondepressed mothers.[6] An increase in depression has also been linked to the perceived inadequacy of social support.[7] In a recent study,[8] social support networks of adult women who had been involved with child welfare for abuse or neglect were compared with social support networks of adult women who had no history of such maltreatment. All women were of low socioeconomic status and matched on significant sociodemographic variables. Maltreating mothers reported they had fewer friends, less contact with friends, and rated the quality of support they received lower than did nonmaltreating mothers. Smithey[9] conducted intensive interviews with women who had killed their children and found that lack of interpersonal support and economic deprivation were precipitating factors for filicide. Smithey described filicidal mothers as having no or little emotional support and indicated that the relationships the women had with others were often emotionally destructive. Smithey found these mothers often resorted to substance abuse. Interestingly, substance abuse frequently preceded abusive interchanges between mothers and children. Although it is unclear whether the women Smithey interviewed killed because of substance abuse, her research provides further support for the importance of situational factors in abusive patterns and the catalyzing effect substances can have on abuse. Similarly, Kelley[10] found that substance-abusing mothers demonstrated more stress and maladaptive parenting behaviors, such as abuse and neglect, than mothers with no known history of substance abuse. In general, mothers with alcohol or drug problems are more likely to be punitive toward their children.[11]

Coohey and Braun suggested that the most potent factors for predicting whether a mother would abuse her child were childhood exposure to aggression and adult domestic violence. They offered a conceptual framework for understanding child abuse that suggested that potential for physical abuse could be mitigated by access to emotional resources.[12] Hall, Sachs, and Rayens[13] also suggested that social resources could diminish a mother's potential for abuse. Clearly, previous and current exposure to violence, the presence of aggravating circumstances, and the availability of resources need to be considered conjointly to understand maternal abuse and maternal filicide stemming from abuse.

The Subcategorization of Abusing Mothers in Previous Typologies

Numerous researchers have suggested that abuse-related maternal filicides represent a unique subcategory of women. Resnick[14] first discussed a subcategory of "accidental" filicide. He suggested that these murders were often the result of "battered child syndrome" and called the deaths accidental because the parent did not intend to kill the child.[15] Bourget and Bradford[16] defined their accidental filicide subcategory the same way and suggested that parents are generally under intense and unusual stress at the time of the fatal incident. d'Orban identified a subgroup of "battering mothers" that included cases in which the killing was the result of "a sudden impulsive act characterized by loss of temper and the immediate stimulus to aggression arose from the victim."[17] d'Orban indicated that the outstanding feature of this group of mothers was their chaotic and often violent home background and accumulation of stressors in their lives. These included intergenerational influences, financial and housing problems, marital violence, and other young children in the home.

More recently, researchers from Australia have also found support for a subcategory of maternal filicide related to abuse. Alder and Baker[18] indicated that women in their fatal assault category faced a number of difficulties, including lack of support, financial and housing problems, and depression. Similarly, Wilczynski[19] found that fatalities in this category often stemmed from attempts to discipline gone awry.

Our Definition and Findings

Our abuse-related filicide category is comprised of mothers whose purposeful physical assault unintentionally led to the child's death. Most of these women had previously assaulted their child or children. None of them purposely killed their child and even the courts recognized this fact, since many were charged with involuntary manslaughter instead of murder. This category can be distinguished from the assisted/coerced category because the mother either acted alone or was primarily responsible for the death.

There were fifteen cases in this category but there was very little information available on three of the cases. The children killed ranged in age from six weeks to six years. However, only two were under a year old. Ten of the women had four or more children. One woman had only one child but none of the remaining fourteen women killed her first-born child. There were approximately equal numbers of male and female victims. All the children but one, who drowned, died as a result of beatings. Almost half of the fatal assaults involved a blow to the head. Although the mothers seemed to abuse all their children, several cases mentioned that the victim seemed to be a target of violence more often than the other children, like Elisa Izquierdo.

Child welfare had previously been involved with twelve of the women and was likely involved with two more, although that was not clear. In two-thirds of the cases the mother had previously lost custody and killed the child after reunification. Although it was unclear how long the mother and child had been reunited, in at least five cases it had been less than six months. Of the five cases that were not reunifications, three of the mothers had previously been reported to child welfare. Because media accounts of the cases did not address domestic violence and mental illness, that information could not be ascertained. Low intellectual functioning was mentioned in two cases.

No one in our sample of mothers was an adolescent, although many were adolescents when they first bore a child. The average age was twenty-seven years old with a range of twenty-one to thirty-nine years old. Substance use was clearly a factor in eight of the cases and at least a third of the victims had been born addicted to substances, but information was not available on the other cases. At least two of the women were pregnant at the time of the killing. Information about the mother's childhood could only be found on two women and both had been exposed to childhood violence. There was virtually no information available on any of the women's perceptions of social support. Also glaringly absent from most of the cases was any discussion of the fathers and their level of involvement with the children. Few of the fathers appeared to reside with the mother.

Social and Policy Issues

An oft-quoted saying, particularly in political arenas, is that it takes a village to raise a child.[20] After Elisa Izquierdo died, responsibility and blame were assigned to everyone and everything in the village. There was blame for her parents, who were being dealt with by the criminal justice system. There was blame for relatives and neighbors, who heard and saw what was happening but did not report it. There was criticism of the multitude of professionals who either did not do their jobs or were remiss in the way they did them. However, the most severe criticism and blame was aimed at the policies and structure of the child welfare system. These criticisms encapsulate many of the key issues related to child welfare policy.

Confidentiality Laws

The first policies to come under attack in the wake of the Elisa Izquierdo case related to the confidentiality of the cases. Criticisms of confidentiality laws were multifaceted but obviously revolved around disclosure of information. The federal Child Abuse Prevention and Treatment Act (CAPTA)[21] which was passed in 1974, emphasized the confidentiality of child welfare records. This law was premised on the notion that juvenile and family court proceedings must be confidential in order to avoid creating stigma and facilitate rehabilitation and treatment. Unfortunately, states' interpretations of the act also often severely limited caseworkers, virtually prohibiting them from discussing a case with many of a child's other providers, such as teachers. After Elisa died, most advocates for child welfare agreed that this aspect of confidentiality should be changed to enable caseworkers and professionals to provide more comprehensive case coverage. This limitation was remedied at both the state and federal levels.

A second set of criticisms concerned disclosure of information related to cases and court proceedings to the general public. Theoretically, such full disclosure would force professionals involved in child welfare cases to be more accountable and could provide an impetus for public involvement, thus promoting reform. New York quickly responded to this call for full disclosure by making family court completely open to the public, although the judge can close the proceeding if there is a compelling reason.[22] Of course, opponents of such disclosure argue that it may not be in the best interests of the child who is being abused and/or his/her siblings. Consider the siblings of Elisa Izquierdo. Pictures and the names of her siblings were readily available in media reports after the confidentiality laws were loosened. Those children may well have been harmed by this breach of privacy. After all, it is quite likely that some of their friends and teachers, neighbors, and acquaintances saw their photographs and read their names in the papers. This violation of the children's privacy may lead to long-term harm as well. These children will one day presumably hold jobs, have their own children, maybe even attempt to adopt or work with children. Allowing information about the abuses they saw and suffered into the public arena could create a severe burden for them.

Alleged abusers could also be harmed when their names are associated with unsubstantiated claims. This latter concern relates to yet another confidentiality consideration. Prior to Elisa's death unsubstantiated claims were sealed or expunged. This procedure may have cost Elisa her life. However, once again, alleged abusers can also be harmed by the maintenance of unfounded reports. A 1996 amendment to CAPTA suggests a middle ground.[23] It discusses the establishment of child abuse and fatality citizen review panels, with provisions for public disclosure when a child dies or nearly dies. Patton[24] further outlines a media access panel to satisfy the need for public disclosure. If one goal of access to information is reform, the establishment of panels made up of committed citizens will more likely facilitate change than broad open access. In states with open proceedings, public interest goes through cycles, peaking after high profile cases but falling at other times. Panels would also meet the goal of holding providers more accountable. Most important, they provide a solution to confidentiality concerns without revictimizing anyone.

Family Reunification/Preservation and Termination of Parental Rights

The child welfare system in New York was also sharply criticized after Elisa Izquierdo's death for its emphasis on family reunification/preservation and the countervailing argument that a parent's rights should be terminated more quickly. Actually, the focus on reunification stems from the enactment in 1980 of the federal Adoption Assistance and Child Welfare Act (AACWA).[25] In the 1970s the theoretical and financial focus of child welfare was on removing children from dangerous homes rather than channeling funding into programs which could have provided services to keep families intact. Of course, this resulted in many children being placed in foster care. The AACWA was created to reverse this trend and provide more permanent solutions, preferably reunification, but also adoption. Child welfare agencies were encouraged to provide more supportive programming for parents which might prevent removal or facilitate reunification, thus decreasing the reliance on foster care. States that complied with the AACWA received federal funding for child welfare programs, including foster care. Not surprisingly, states became strong advocates for reunification.

The AACWA indicated that states were to make efforts at reunification, but these efforts were not defined nor were time limits set for rehabilitation. Consequently, child welfare bureaus made extensive efforts so as not to lose funding. The number of children in foster care continued to rise while exhaustive attempts were made to rehabilitate families through services aimed at family reunification, such as parent education, counseling, or day care. Unfortunately, these programs are not perfect and parents may complete them, but nonetheless fail to be rehabilitated prior to being reunited with their children. Additionally, follow-up services were often not provided after reunification, when parents needed them most. Some services were never made available at all. Nevertheless, efforts at rehabilitation and reunification continued even when they seemed to conflict with the best interests of the child. Foster placements had revolving doors whereby children were reunited only to be returned to a new foster home, and then be reunited again and returned to another foster home.

Further compounding the problem, until reasonable efforts had been made the court was unlikely to agree to terminate parental rights, thus freeing a child for adoption. In the meantime, federal funding paid for foster care placements. So even if there were a prospective adoptive parent, s/he would have to wait until all reunification efforts had been exhausted. This could take years, since no time limits were defined. Then if the parents did not give up parental rights, the court would have to be convinced that all reunification efforts had been made before terminating parental rights and clearing the way for adoption proceedings.

Elisa Izquierdo was likely caught up in the heroic reunification efforts of the child welfare bureau, despite the fact that her mother should not have been considered a candidate for reunification. Soon after her death, states begun to set limits so children could be adopted out more quickly.[26] Federal legislation designed to result in quicker termination of parental rights was also enacted in 1997. The Adoption and Safe Families Act (ASFA) directs child welfare agencies to focus on the child's health and safety, not on the family as a whole.[27] The goal of ASFA is to increase adoptions. To this end, the ASFA encourages states to terminate rights more quickly by placing time limits on family reunification, giving states financial incentives for increased adoption rates, and waiving the reasonable efforts standard in extreme cases.

However, calling for a quick termination of parental rights is shortsighted. The majority of children (up to 90 percent in come areas) removed from parental homes do not suffer from abuse but from neglect.[28] The neglect is usually the result of poverty. Terminating parental rights more quickly would adversely affect these families without addressing the real problem, which is poverty. Since a disproportionate number of families involved with the child welfare system are families of color, terminating parental rights more quickly would result in destabilizing homes that are already impacted by racism at other levels. In addition, some families of color became involved in the child welfare system because of discriminatory practices. This could be due to the racial bias of child welfare workers and/or the difficulties and ambiguities inherent in defining abuse and neglect. This is further exaggerated by a general lack of ethnocultural understanding and training on the part of child welfare workers.

In sum, the majority of families impacted by a quicker termination of parental rights would be families whose children are removed because of neglect. Quick termination does not solve the problem of poverty, often the source of the neglect, and may result in disparate treatment of families with low socioeconomic status and families of color. ASFA would have helped Elisa Izquierdo and may help with many child abuse cases, but it could also be incredibly harmful to families and children who have been separated because of neglect.

Moreover, a quicker termination may not benefit children. After termination, children simply end up in an overburdened foster care system with no links to anyone, and now with no family name. This is not to say that a parent's rights should not be terminated. However, once it is clear the family cannot be reunited, unless relatives or foster parents are petitioning for adoption, children will be in foster care whether the parents' rights are terminated or not. The focus should be on increasing adoption options before severing family ties so that a new link is readily available for children when family ties are severed. Unfortunately, in general there is a scarcity of adoptive parents.

Conna Craig, founder of the Institute for Children in Massachusetts and a former child of foster care, believes the foster care system creates financial incentives for foster parents with no parallel incentives for adoptive parents.[29] Craig created an adoption program that included legal reforms, computerized tracking of children available for adoption, and aggressive recruiting of adoptive families.[30] Her program was extremely successful in Massachusetts. It is based on the premise that all children are adoptable. Craig also supports turning adoptions over to private agencies to enhance competition.[31] In addition, she suggests we reexamine the taboos against transracial adoption, which have created obstacles to providing families for minority children.

The issue of transracial adoption became a major consideration after the National Association of Black Social Workers published a position paper in 1972 criticizing transracial adoption and indicating that black children should be raised in black families.[32] Thereafter child welfare agencies and private adoption centers increased their scrutiny of families considering transracial adoptions. This has resulted in both positive and negative outcomes.

One very positive outcome is that social workers involved with adoptions have incorporated readings and discussion of transracial issues into their home study evaluation and education. Correspondingly, families considering transracial adoptions are more aware of and better educated regarding the need to become involved in and promote identification with a child's ethnocultural heritage. Unfortunately, a negative outcome is that some public agencies may have actively discouraged or delayed transracial adoption, leaving some children to languish in foster care. Moreover, the underlying issue remains the same. It would be hard to argue that families of color are less concerned about keeping their families intact or have less love for their children than white families. So many children of color would not be available for adoption if institutionalized racism was not so prevalent in our society. Although adopting children out will address the immediate crisis of an overburdened foster care system, it does nothing to address issues such as educational disparity and discrimination, which may be at the root of the entire problem.

It is too early to determine the impact of ASFA. The director of New York's child welfare agency, Nicholas Scoppetta, who was appointed in response to Elisa Izquierdo's death, said he was proud that his agency had helped family court process 18,500 adoptions in the last five years. Although admirable, these statistics also reflect a national increase in both the number of children in foster care and the number of children adopted from foster care.[33] From 1998 to 1999 there was a 28 percent national increase in the number of foster care children adopted.[34] Not surprisingly, the increase in the number of adoptions has corresponded with an increase in federal "bonus" funding for each child adopted out of foster care, even if that adoption is later reversed.[35] Without more judges and lawyers, increases in adoptions will likely begin to stress an already overburdened judicial system.

Inadequacies of the Child Welfare System

There is little dispute that the child welfare system in New York was woefully inadequate at the time of Elisa Izquierdo's death. Critics identified many problems ranging from high caseloads to the lack of computer systems. These are typical criticisms of most child welfare systems and are outlined below along with updates regarding the success of New York's attempts at reform. Positive changes in any of the following areas would make intervention both more likely to occur and more effective.

CASELOAD TOO HIGH AND LACK OF SUPERVISION

During the year that Elisa Izquierdo's caseworker managed her case, he was also responsible for anywhere from twenty-five to thirty-seven other cases.[36] Each case can require several hours of work each week in case management, visits, paperwork, and hearings. At the time, the standards for the New York child welfare agency stated that no more than fifteen cases can be handled safely at any one time.[37] In June 1996 the average caseload for New York was twenty-seven.[38] In November 2000 the average had been reduced to thirteen. This was probably the result of Mayor Giuliani providing funding to hire two hundred casework-ers.[39] However, across the country overburdened child welfare agencies are the rule, not the exception, and this is particularly problematic in rural areas where caseworkers spend a significant amount of time trav-eling to homes.

SYSTEM OUTDATED AND RECORDS LOST

When Elisa moved from one part of town to another, her records were not transferred from her initial child welfare worker to her new child welfare worker. In fact, they appeared to be lost. Even after her death, the records that were available were incomplete. In fact, when a general audit of the agency was conducted in April 1996, caseworkers were un-able to produce 14 percent of the records which auditors requested.[40] Caseworkers blamed this poor record keeping partially on a lack of ac-cess to technology, maintaining they had no access to computers or even voicemail. Today New York caseworkers have voicemail and computers and each case is reportedly charted and graphed.

INADEQUATE TRAINING

Criticisms of child welfare systems include inadequate training in record keeping practices, and inadequate education and awareness about multicultural issues, child neglect, and child abuse and abusers (in-cluding being able to identify warning signs). In April 1996 New York auditors found violations of procedure in 78 percent of the cases they re-viewed.[41] Moreover, only 62 percent of the cases that had been closed merited that determination and 18 percent of the cases should have re-mained open because of the risk of child abuse.[42] By November 1996 New York had increased training significantly for both new and experi-enced caseworkers, including five more days of initial training, on-the-job-training, and refresher training after six months. Experienced case-workers received additional training in risk assessment.

SERVICES NOT PROVIDED OR NOT PROVIDED LONG ENOUGH

Services were never clearly defined under the AACWA, although suggestions were offered. It is clear that services need to be offered relating to prevention of abuse, support, and parental education and that they need to be offered for extended periods of time. Although New York identified this need, as of November 2000, "Basic services used to prevent or treat child abuse—domestic violence counseling, translators, drug abuse programs—are in short supply in some parts of the city."[43]

INADEQUATE PAY AND HIRING

One of the problems caused by inadequate pay is that there is an incredibly high turnover rate among caseworkers, reducing stability and continuity for families who are already unstable. In addition, the longer a caseworker is involved with a family the greater the disclosure and the more likely it is that abusive or neglectful patterns will be identified. In 1996, the starting salary for caseworkers in New York was $26,000, with no salary increase for ten years unless the caseworker was promoted to supervisor. The turnover rate was 49 percent.[44] Base salaries in 2000 were $37,000, with merit raises that allow an individual to earn up to $52,000. It is unclear how this has impacted turnover.

THE INADEQUACIES OF FAMILY COURTS

Family courts are frequently criticized for having an insufficient number of judges and attorneys and for their overall lack of training in the psychological and social aspects of family systems. Even though the number of family court cases in New York increased from 182,201 in 1990 to 226,309 in 1996, there were still only forty-seven judges.[45] In 1997, judges handled an average of 3,300 cases a year.[46] In a 1998 law review Bailie argued that given the movement away from profamily legislation represented by ASFA, parents in poverty are even more in need of competent legal representation.[47] Representation varies across states but many indigent parents may meet their court-appointed attorney at their hearing. Moreover, their attorney may be a public defender who has no experience in neglect proceedings but is trained in criminal defense practices. Bailie argues that competent representation can correct the imbalance of power facing parents in child protective proceedings, help parents navigate the child welfare system, and provide advocacy.

Clearly, the current family court system does not represent anyone's interests well—neither the state, nor the parents, nor the child. In addition to the inadequacies outlined by Bailie, court personnel are in dire need of multicultural awareness training and education.

The New York child welfare system has been closely scrutinized since the death of Elisa Izquierdo and has focused attention on addressing inadequacies. The changes they have been able to implement in five years are impressive and support the notion that reforms can come about quickly. However, even with this increased emphasis, the New York system has only been able to address some criticisms and it is unclear whether the changes have had any impact. Moreover, the New York model is not representative of most of the child welfare systems in the country.

In November 2000, the lead article on the cover of *Time* magazine was entitled "The Crisis of Foster Care."[48] The article begins with numerous stories of child abuse in the foster care system, generally by *foster* parents or families. However, the abuses within foster homes are compounded by failures in the child welfare system. The authors focus on three states where they maintain the foster care system is failing; Georgia, Alabama, and California. But they argue it is in a crisis nationwide with lawyers threatening class action suits in twenty states. They report that the number of children in foster care has doubled in the last five years (1995 to 2000) from approximately one quarter of a million to half a million. Agencies are plagued with poor and outdated record keeping and unmanageable records as well as inadequate case monitoring, bad decisions, high turnover (as much as 70 percent), poorly trained staff, and low accountability. Many problems are noted to be the result of decentralization. Although the federal government sets standards and provides funding, the states are left to regulate their own child welfare systems. In turn, states often turn this responsibility over to the counties. The counties can create policies and systems that are at best burdensome or inefficient and at worst, infringe on individual rights.

Band-Aids

When a child like Elisa Izquierdo dies under tragic circumstances, sweeping legislation like ASFA is often quickly enacted. The legislation does not provide a solution but a Band-Aid and often violates individual rights. All too frequently these are women's rights. Consider the following policy.

When Rozanne Perkins beat her two-year-old son Davon to death in Dayton, Ohio, it was quickly brought to light that she had had previous involvement with both the criminal justice and child welfare systems. Perkins children had previously been removed from her home and she had had child endangerment and domestic violence charges filed against her in the past, although she was not convicted of either charge. Montgomery County (in which Dayton, Ohio, is located) quickly enacted a policy whereby prosecutors can file dependency complaints whenever a baby is born to parents who have had other children removed from their home due to abuse or neglect.[49] Within two months nine babies had been removed from their homes and ten families were receiving counseling. Moreover, "officials are considering expanding the Prosecutor's policy to include children born before it was implemented. In addition, several agencies have been working for the past four months to develop a 'red flag' policy to intervene with parents dealing with substance abuse, domestic violence or other issues that put them at risk of endangering their children."[50]

On the surface this appears to be a well-intended policy. However, it has a fatal procedural flaw in that there is no standard mechanism to inform the child welfare bureau when a previously neglectful or abusive parent becomes a new parent. Therefore, families referred under the policy were largely identified by agencies that generally provide services to low-income families. Unfortunately, the families referred are using the services and families who are needing the services but not using them are not identified. This punishes those families who seek assistance. Moreover, under a such a policy mothers are much more likely to come to the attention of the child welfare bureau since they have more exposure to healthcare systems during pregnancies and childbirth. A man could quite easily slip through the cracks in the system. Finally, recall that most child welfare cases are cases of neglect, not abuse. It would be hard to argue that Perkins does not need some kind of monitoring (and so does the father of Davon who was at best neglectful but would not likely be referred under this policy). However, does the family who suffered a difficult financial time need to be monitored forever even after they have achieved financial stability? Doesn't that violate their right to privacy? In addition, in a system which is overburdened and financially limited, how will this new monitoring be accomplished? Unfortunately, bad policies and legislation often remain in place because the people most affected by them are least able to challenge them. Legislation, like reforms of the system, are only Band-Aids that mask the underlying causes of many cases of abuse and neglect, namely, impoverished conditions.

Community Involvement

There have been numerous excellent attempts to garner grassroots community involvement in existing programs or program development.

New York is attempting to implement neighborhood-based child welfare services.[51] Under this program troubled neighborhoods would be identified and local private agencies would be appointed to work with families. The child welfare agency would investigate abuse and pay the bill for services.[52] Involving private agencies to provide services has the benefit of increasing providers. However, it also increases the number of agencies that must be monitored, making the system more vulnerable to mismanagement due to lack of supervision over the agencies. In 2000, a state inspection of the Colorado foster system revealed that officials had given up trying to inspect the multitude of privately run child-placement agencies.[53] In the end, privatization may jeopardize the safety of children. Citizen watches have also been proposed and supported. New York has agreed to give an outside community agency full access to child welfare records to serve as a type of overseer.[54] Involving an ombudsman has also been proposed by other child welfare agencies.

In March 2000 the Wisconsin legislature passed a bill to allow volunteers to be trained, to maintain regular contact with children who had been abused, and to monitor their home life.[55] The measure allows the volunteers to interview the children without parental consent. The program is an offshoot of the Court Appointed Special Advocate Program, and some Wisconsin counties are already using it in a modified form. Although there are multiple problems inherent in such an intervention, it is refreshing to see programs that facilitate community involvement as opposed to legislative prohibitions and sanctions.

In yet another proposal, it was suggested that schools either hire a social worker or redefine the role of an existing school counselor such that his/her sole purpose would be to act as a liaison with child welfare. This person would be responsible for reporting suspected child abuse to child welfare and act as a contact for child welfare when reports came to their attention, thus providing more collaborative services. Such a liaison would probably have saved the life of Elisa Izquierdo.

The goal of all these programs is to allocate more responsibilities to inner systems, including schools, families, and communities, making the village more responsible for raising the child. However, in the end it is not the innovativeness of the program as much as the commitment of the community and individuals within the community that insures that programs are implemented and monitored to facilitate success. In Georgia and Alabama, well-designed reforms were either partially implemented or implemented but not monitored.[56] The result is a failed system.

Epilogue

Featherstone[57] suggests that mothers who abuse their children are frequently viewed as either victims or villains, either totally powerless or totally powerful. Perhaps the abuse is their way of obtaining the illusion of power and control. However, mothers who kill their children, especially through abuse, represent a total lack of control and power.

Given all the reforms implemented in New York and the raising of public awareness (and presumably consciousness), it was disheartening when Daytwon Bennett died there on March 29, 1997, from beatings and starvation. His mother had taken the five-year-old to the hospital claiming he had a stomach virus. Daytwon had rope and cigarette burns, lacerations, puncture wounds, scars, bruises, and welts all over his body. Apparently, he had spent his last day tied to a chair while his mother beat him with a broomstick. Daytwon had been punished repeatedly for stealing bottles from a younger sibling in an effort to obtain nourishment. His body was the size of a three-year-old's.

Daytwon's mother, Jocelyn Bennett, first lost custody of her children in 1989. She regained and lost custody numerous times during the next eight years. There were many reported incidents involving scalding and/or beating. In June 1996, she regained custody of Daytwon and her five other sons after undergoing counseling. As a condition of the reunification, she was to continue counseling.

Jocelyn's caseworker was diligent about visiting the home, with thirteen visits over the next eight months. However, on those visits she did not check for bruises or interview Daytwon alone, as required. Unfortunately, she also did not follow-up on Jocelyn's counseling attendance. A month before the boy died, the caseworker found him to be small but not malnourished. Nine days before he died the caseworker visited but Jocelyn said Daytwon was unavailable because he was with his father. Although many neighbors thought Jocelyn was abusing the children, they did not report it.

Jocelyn pled guilty to second-degree murder. She indicated that she had pled guilty to spare her children from testifying. She was sentenced to seventeen years to life. Again the system was criticized. Although training had improved and the caseload had decreased since the Elisa Izquierdo case, critics were still concerned about the quality of services. In the meantime, Bennett's six children, including one she had while in prison, are working their way through the foster care system.

As of August 1998, Awilda Lopez's five remaining children were also still wending their way through New York's foster care system. Awilda retained legal rights to the children. Officials had not yet attempted to terminate parental rights. In the meantime, it was difficult to find a placement for a large group of siblings, particularly when they had all likely been psychologically traumatized. Three of the siblings were living together but the older two lived in separate homes. Most of them had moved repeatedly. The oldest boy did not want to be adopted. No one was interested in adopting the oldest girl. Someone is interested in adopting the three youngest siblings but the adoption will reportedly take years.

6

ASSISTANCE OR COERCION
FROM A PARTNER

Relations to Domestic Violence

❑

Sherain Bryant, thirty-eight, and her husband Orlando Bryant, fifty-one, had twice lost custody of their five children prior to the beating death of their daughter Shayna, four. Shayna's siblings testified at the trial that their parents frequently beat the children, tied them to chairs overnight, and burned them with cigarettes. Shayna, they reported, always received the most severe abuse because their mother "hated her and said she was ugly." On the night of her death, Shayna was made to drink water from the toilet and was subsequently beaten in a "bloody room-to-room journey" that resulted in her lying crumpled on the kitchen table.

Urbelina Emiliano, twenty-two, and her husband, Fortino Perez, twenty-seven, were convicted of burying alive Emiliano's two-day-old daughter in order to spare Perez the shame of raising another man's child. Emiliano was seven months pregnant when she married Perez, her childhood sweetheart from their native Mexican village. Emiliano testified that her husband took the baby from her, buried it alive against her will, then assaulted and raped her, and told her not to tell anyone. She reports that she was unable to report the death because her husband kept her bound and gagged each day when he went to work. She also feared for her own safety. Both were convicted of second-degree murder.

Despite numerous differences, the above cases of maternal filicide have an important factor in common: the involvement of the mother's partner. This factor is noteworthy because research indicates that most women who kill their children act alone. According to a 1995 study by researchers at the University of South Carolina, parents are to blame half to three-quarters of the time when children are killed. All the mothers killed alone and most killed in their home.[1] In fact, the majority of filicide research focuses on women who act alone. A review of the literature yielded only one study that mentioned women who kill their children with the aid of a partner, and said it did so only to indicate that they had been excluded from that particular study.[2] Consequently, very little is known about women who kill their children with the assistance or coercion of a partner.

Such women represent a small but significant population. As the current chapter will demonstrate, the characterization of women in this category is unlike that of women in other categories. Unique markers characterize this group of women: most notably, they tend to be involved with abusive, violent male partners during the period in which they kill their children.

The nature of the violence within these relationships is crucial to understanding the circumstances of the children's deaths. The violence perpetrated by the women's partners is not comprised of isolated, aggressive events. Rather, the men's behavior constitutes domestic violence, which includes multiple types of abuse (i.e., physical, psychological, and sexual) occurring in a cycle that often increases in frequency and intensity.[3] Battering relationships may involve abuse in any or all of four different areas: physical (i.e., hitting, pushing, restraining, using a weapon), sexual (i.e., raping, forcing sexual acts by use of physical or emotional manipulation), destruction of pets and property (i.e., abusing pets, breaking furniture, destroying valued possessions), and psychological (i.e., making threats, controlling all the money, ridiculing). Relationships may vary according to type and severity of abuse, but the abuse is always intended to control and to invoke fear in the victims.[4] This repetitive pattern of abuse greatly influenced the behavior of the women in the partner-assisted category. If not for the abusiveness of the men in this sample, the children may very well still be alive. This factor alone makes the partner-assisted category very different from the other categories of maternal filicide. Thus, this chapter fills a much-needed gap in the filicide literature.

Our research identified twelve cases committed between 1990 and 1999 that fit the profile of partner-involved maternal filicide. We have subdivided these cases into two categories: active and passive. Five cases were assigned to the active subcategory, in which women were directly involved in their children's deaths. Seven cases were placed in the passive category, in which women were charged with their children's deaths due to their inability to protect their children. The number of cases included in this category is much lower than those included in most of the other chapters in this book and is probably an underestimate of the actual number of partner-involved maternal filicides. In fact, we found multiple cases that appeared to be partner-involved but which we were unable to classify due to lack of information. We believe that the paucity in the literature with regard to partner-involved cases is noteworthy. As discussed later in this chapter, society generally holds mothers, rather than fathers, responsible for their children's safety and well-being, which may increase the media's tendency to discount fathers' participation. It is likely, therefore, that some cases of partner-involved maternal filicide are either not covered by the media or are misleading because the partner's involvement is not mentioned.

This chapter will provide a comprehensive description of the previously overlooked partner-involved category of maternal filicide. The following section provides an overview of the dynamics of domestic violence. We then present a detailed description of the first category of

partner-assisted infanticide, namely, cases involving the active participation of the mother. Next we describe the second category of cases,
which includes women who were convicted for failing to save their children from their partners' abuse. We discuss the way in which the criminal justice system views these cases and theorize about the justice system's assignment of blame. We close this chapter with policy suggestions for preventing this particular form of infanticide.

An Overview of the Dynamics of Domestic Violence

Stereotypes suggest that women involved with violent men are poor,
uneducated, passive individuals who must enjoy the abuse because if
they did not they would leave the men.[5] Despite these common beliefs,
decades of research indicate that there is no personality profile of a battered woman. She is not necessarily poor or uneducated, although these
factors can certainly contribute to a woman's ability to end an abusive
relationship. Neither is she weak, dependent, or masochistic. Instead, a
battered woman can be anyone.[6] Indeed, the leading cause of injury to
women is domestic violence.[7] More women are hurt by male partners
than are hurt in auto accidents, rapes, or muggings.[8] In fact, domestic
violence is so prevalent that in the mid-1980s the U.S. Centers for Disease Control began considering it an epidemic. Data collected by the
Federal Bureau of Investigation (FBI) from 1979 to 1987 indicate that
women were victims of 5.6 million violent attacks by their male partners, an annual average of 626,000 per year.[9] A woman is beaten every
fifteen seconds and half of all couples have had at least one violent incident.[10] These numbers are probably conservative since as much as 91
percent of intimate abuse may never be reported.[11]

Perhaps the first question that comes to many people's minds when
they hear about a woman being battered is: "Why doesn't she leave?"
Given the tremendous number of women who are abused by an intimate
partner, it seems likely that there are powerful reasons that prevent a

woman from leaving a battering relationship. Domestic violence theory and research indicates that there are, indeed, strong social, political, and psychological factors motivating women to stay in abusive relationships. In fact, there is much evidence to suggest that women are taught to remain in battering relationships, both through typical socialization processes and through exposure to the abuse itself.[12]

Male-female socialization and sex-role stereotyping have a tremendous influence on women's difficulty in leaving abusive relationships. In American culture, women's identity is formed through their attachments to others. A woman's sense of self is dependent on her ability to connect with and affiliate with others. While masculinity is characterized by independence, strength, and powerfulness, femininity is defined by dependence, selflessness, and passivity. Many women can recall both subtle and overt cultural and familial messages suggesting that disagreement or conflict are unacceptable, "unladylike" behaviors for women.[13] Thus, when a woman defies cultural expectations, whether by taking a job promotion, expressing anger, or leaving an intimate relationship, she risks being chastised by others and losing her identity as a woman. Our societal expectations, then, place a tremendous burden on women who have violent partners. Although they are harshly judged and criticized for staying with a violent partner, so too are women blamed for leaving because they have "broken up" their marriage or deprived their children of a father.[14] It is not difficult to understand why women might endure abuse rather than defy cultural norms that define their identity as a female.

In addition to socialization patterns that teach women to stay in abusive relationships, the abuse itself often poses a tremendous stay or leave dilemma for women. One well-accepted theory of why women stay is Lenore Walker's "Cycle of Violence Theory."[15] Walker describes domestic violence as a cycle consisting of three phases. The first phase, tension building, involves a buildup of anger and "minor" incidents of violence such as name-calling, threats, and breaking things. This phase escalates to the second one, that of acute battering, in which "major" violence such as physical abuse occurs. The third phase, the honeymoon phase, occurs last. During this period the batterer is remorseful and contrite. He may beg his partner to stay with him, make promises, bring gifts, and behave in a loving manner.

It is the honeymoon phase that explains why many women stay with abusive men. This honeymoon phase provides hope. During this period, the woman regards the batterer as the "real" man with whom she initially fell in love. It allows a battered woman to believe that her partner will change his abusive behavior.[16] She needs this hope because a change in her partner's behavior is the only satisfactory resolution to the situation. She will be blamed whether she stays or leaves the abusive relationship. However, if the abuse were to end, her identity as a "good" partner and "good" woman would be reaffirmed. Women receive much support in their hope that a violent partner may change his behavior. The idea that it is possible (and even expected) for women to change their male partners is reinforced by literature, song lyrics, religion, the media, family, and friends.[17]

There are countless other reasons why women remain with abusive partners. Women cite reasons such as religious convictions and the desire to honor legal commitments. Lack of alternatives also prevents them from leaving. Many women do not have the economic resources to leave. Some, in an effort to fulfill their identity as a good woman, have sacrificed their own careers in order to support their partner's career or to raise their children. They may therefore not have the financial or vocational resources to leave a violent partner. Additionally, many women do not have adequate social support.[18] They have no one to turn to for help. Families in the United States are more isolated than ever before. Many couples live at a great distance from extended family. Although domestic violence shelters provide an option for some women, there are not enough shelters to assist all the women who need them. Further, these shelters typically offer only a temporary respite, not a long-term solution.[19]

Fear is another reason why women stay in abusive relationships.

Research consistently shows that the end of a relationship is the most dangerous time for a woman and her children.[20] Women often report that their abusive partner has threatened to harm or kill them or their children if they leave.[21] Law enforcement officials and the justice system provide little or no assistance to battered women. If a woman seeks help from the police, she risks being arrested herself because batterers are frequently convincing in their attempts to blame their partners for the abuse. She may even have her children taken from her, as battered women are frequently perceived to be unfit parents. Further, the courts generally offer little protection to women attempting to leave violent partners. Abusing a loved one is considered less of a crime than behaving aggressively toward a stranger. Restraining orders are often not enforced, as domestic violence continues to be considered a "private" issue that should be resolved within the family.[22] Seeking legal assistance or leaving the relationship may therefore simply result in greater risk for a woman and her children.

It is not difficult to understand how being trapped in a violent relationship, repeatedly subjected to abuse, and receiving no cultural or legal support frequently takes a toll on women. Research indicates that involvement in a violent relationship often leads to similar kinds of stress reactions as exposure to war or other traumas. Symptoms may include shock, disorientation, passivity, exaggerated startle response, numbing, and lack of interest in one's activities. The domestic violence literature suggests that approximately 45 percent of battered women meet the full criteria for Posttraumatic Stress Disorder, an anxiety disorder resulting from prolonged exposure to a traumatic event. Stress reactions resulting from domestic violence may be particularly severe because the abuse is unpredictable. This unpredictability leads women to feel helpless which, in turn, increases their level of stress.[23]

Another possible consequence of domestic violence is increased aggressiveness on the part of the victim. Research with both animals and humans demonstrates that punishment leads to increased aggression.

For example, a punished monkey will attack objects, other animals, even itself. Humans subjected to shocks in laboratory experiments become aggressive as well. Therefore, it is not surprising that people who are continually battered may eventually experience a buildup of aggression themselves. Being in a chronically violent situation provides an explanation for why some battered women batter their children.[24] As it would be incredibly unsafe for women to retaliate against their batterers, some women turn their anger and helplessness toward their children. Research indicates that battered women are more likely to abuse their children than are other mothers, although much less frequently than batterers.[25] Further, a battered woman may exhaust all her resources "tiptoeing" around the batterer, attempting to predict and prevent the next episode of violence. She may simply not have any patience or reason left to deal with a screaming toddler or ornery preschooler.

The domestic violence literature helps us understand the unique profiles of women in the active as well as passive partner-involved infanticide category. We will describe the characterizations of women in these categories and will discuss the relevance of domestic violence research to the circumstances of these cases. We begin with the active partner-involved cases.

Active Partner-Involved Infanticide

Sharon Burton, thirty-two, was charged with murder following the drowning death of her daughter Dominique Spencer, three. Police detectives report that Burton's boyfriend, Leroy Locke, forty-seven, with the consent of Burton, submerged Dominique's head in a bathtub filled with water because the child was having difficulties with toilet training. Police stated that Dominique was beaten repeatedly by her mother before she drowned. According to the Illinois Department of Children and Family Services, the child had been born with drugs in her system.

Women in the active partner-involved infanticide category are older than many women who kill their children. They were an average of 26.2 years old when their children were killed. This age is surprisingly high: A common explanation for maternal filicide is that the mothers are young, immature, and less able to handle pressure. For example, a study examining all births in the United States between 1983 and 1991 found that the mother's age was one of the most important risk factors for infant homicide. Children born to women younger than age nineteen were most at risk.[26]

Although our data support the literature which suggests that the majority of women who kill their children are young, we have also found that three filicide categories, namely abuse-related, purposeful, and partner-involved cases, consist of women who are older. This suggests that maternal filicide may not always be related to immaturity and inexperience.

A second important aspect of the partner-involved filicide category is the partner's relationship to the child. A large percentage (43 percent) of the partners in this sample were not the biological parent of the child killed. The literature suggests that children are more at risk of being harmed by caretakers who are not biologically related. For example, in a study of children younger than five murdered in Philadelphia during 1993 and the first half of 1994, researchers found that the children were more likely to be killed by their mothers' boyfriends serving as babysitters than by their mothers or fathers.[27]

A third finding in this category is that a significant percentage of women report being abused by their partners. Of the five cases in this category, two women reported that they were battered by their partners. This is not surprising, as the majority of abusive men abuse both their partners and the partners' children.[28] An interesting finding is that the women's partners were an average of 8.4 years older than they were. In three of the cases, the partners were twelve to fifteen years older than the women.

Several other notable aspects of this category are social context, method of death, and age of the child. The majority of women in this sample were experiencing multiple social stressors, including poverty and the presence of multiple children in the home. The deaths of their children typically resulted from discipline-related abuse that escalated into death. All the children in this sample had been physically abused. Numerous women reported that the death occurred during their attempts to discipline the child. They had not actually intended to kill the child, as the use of a gun or more lethal method of killing (i.e., hanging, fire) might suggest. Instead, the majority of the deaths resulted from beatings. These incidents appear to have occurred during times that are typically stressful for parents. For instance, Sherain Bryant and Sharon Burton are both reported to have killed their children during toileting accidents. Overwhelming stressors and lack of resources likely contributed to the women's difficulty in tempering their attempts to discipline.

Children in this sample were an average of 27.8 months old when they were killed. According to the maternal filicide literature, young children are more likely than older children to be murdered by their mothers. For example, half of all abuse or neglect-related deaths involve children younger than age one.[29] One hypothesis for the greater percentage of young children killed is that young children are more demanding and frustrating than older children. Infants require an enormous amount of care, are too young to understand rules or instructions, and may cry for what appears to be "no reason." Further, young children progress through numerous developmental stages (i.e., toilet training, the "terrible twos") that may be frustrating for parents.

A second hypothesis for the higher prevalence of young children killed is that they are more vulnerable than older children. The physical abuse required to kill an infant may be much less than that needed to kill an older child. Parents may not be aware of the vulnerability of young children. For example, many parents shake their infants and unknowingly cause brain injury or death.[30]

To sum up, women in this category tend to be older than the average woman who kills her child, and are involved with abusive older men who are not biologically related to their children. They are typically coping with multiple social stressors, including the presence of young children in the home. The deaths of their children generally result from discipline gone awry, during a stressful incident such as a toileting accident.

The large age discrepancy between the women and their partners is striking and may certainly have contributed to the power differential in their relationships. Abusive men generally have underlying feelings of insecurity and vulnerability. In order to combat these feelings, they seek power and control.[31] Selecting a much younger partner can help fulfill their need to feel strong and powerful. The insecurity of abusive men also leads to frequent bouts of intense jealousy.[32] The presence of a child who is not biologically their own probably serves as a powerful reminder that their female partner had previously been involved with another man. Their abuse toward the child may have been related to this jealousy. The women in this category may have subtly or overtly been expected to abuse the child as well, as a way of proving their loyalty to their partner. Some women may even have abused their child in order to spare the child more severe abuse from their partners.

In the next section we turn to a second category of partner-involved maternal filicide, that in which the woman did not have an active role in her child's death. Women in the passive partner-involved category are both similar to, and different from, those in the active partner-involved category.

Passive Partner-Involved Infanticide

Pauline Zile, twenty-four, was found guilty of first-degree murder in the beating death of her seven-year-old daughter Christina Holt. Zile, however, did not kill her daughter. She was convicted, rather, for "failure to protect" her daughter. Her husband, John Zile, reportedly beat his stepdaughter because of a toileting accident. He had a history of alleged abuse of Christina, including beatings, torture, humiliation, even dropping her off in a dangerous part of town to "teach her a lesson" about running away. Following Christina's death, John Zile put her body in a closet for four days, then buried her in an empty lot. The Ziles then told police that she had been kidnaped. Within a week, Mrs. Zile confessed to police.

We have previously discussed the multiple factors that prevent women from leaving battering relationships. The active category of partner-assisted infanticide involved battered women whose fear, helplessness, and anger came to be directed toward their children. These cases are relatively infrequent. More common are situations in which women do not behave violently toward their children but are blamed for their inability to prevent their partner from abusing the children.

As a culture, we blame women for these deaths. We, the authors of this book, believe that women are blamed because our culture expects a battered woman to select one of two options: leave the batterer or stop the abuse occurring within the relationship. When she is unable to do either, we hold her responsible for abuse that befalls her and her children.

We have previously described the multiple social, political, and psychological reasons that prevent a woman from leaving an abusive man. However, we have not yet mentioned the sometimes subtle, even unconscious, tendency we have of blaming women for domestic violence. Much attention has been paid in recent years to the "blame the victim" phenomenon that often occurs in situations involving rape. When hearing of a rape, we may ask ourselves, "What was she doing in that neighborhood anyway?" or "Why was she wearing that short skirt?" Such questions make it the victim's responsibility to prove that she did not ask for or elicit the rape, instead of holding the perpetrator responsible for his actions. We blame the victim in other situations as well. Barnett and LaViolette[33] point out, for example, that we may hold people accountable for being burglarized because they did not have better locks on their doors. Similarly, we may wonder whether the victim of a drive-by shooting was an innocent bystander or a gang member.

We hold battered women responsible in the same way. We ask ourselves what they did to elicit such abuse. We argue that no one is solely to blame when a relationship runs into difficulties ("it takes two to tango"). Consequently, a battered woman must have done something, or must be flawed in some way, for her partner to have been angry enough to behave so aggressively toward her. And if the woman is partly responsible for the abuse, then it follows that she can do something to stop it.

Our tendency to hold women responsible for domestic violence is even greater when children are involved. Society paints a rosy picture of motherhood. Mothers are supposed to be loving, self-sacrificing, and patient. Motherhood is supposed to be a woman's greatest aspiration and women are therefore expected to protect their children under any circumstance. Fatherhood is not viewed in the same way. Although many people do not condone fathers abusing their children, a father's primary role does not involve protecting and nurturing children. Men are allowed to have aspirations and roles beyond fatherhood. Consequently, a man who fails to protect his children is not necessarily a failure as a person. Women who "allow" their children to be hurt, on the other hand, have failed at their most fundamental responsibility.[34]

The blame the victim phenomenon serves an important purpose. It allows us to believe that we are safe from such atrocities. We will never be burglarized, or raped, or abused by a partner because we will do things the *right* way. Believing that the world is just and that people get what they deserve allows us to exclude ourselves from the possibility of tragedy. However, the reality is that women who are victims of intimate abuse can often do very little to stop the abuse from occurring. Battered women generally "walk on eggshells" around their partner, attempting to predict and prevent future abuse. However, research indicates that most women cannot predict the timing of abuse. Batterers purposely behave unpredictably as a means of increasing their power and control within the relationship.[35] The vast majority of abusive men have been abusive in multiple relationships, further indicating that the abuse results from their own issues rather than from the behavior of their female partners.[36]

The profile of women in the passive partner-assisted infanticide category is consistent with the domestic violence literature. There are similarities between these women and the women in the active partner-assisted category; however, women in this category did not abuse their children themselves. Rather, they were unable to prevent their partner from harming the child and may not have accurately reported the death to authorities. Women in this category are also younger than women who had a more active role in their child's death. The average age of the women in this sample is 23.0 years (data not available for one of the women). Women in this subcategory, therefore, appear to be closer in age to the majority of women who kill their children. They may be especially inexperienced and vulnerable to control.

Indeed, information about the women's partners reveals that the presence of a partner had a significant impact on the situation. Domestic violence was extremely prevalent in this subgroup. Urbelina Emiliano, for example, reported that she feared for her own safety as the result of repeated physical and sexual assaults and verbal threats from her husband. She stated that when she tried to save her child from being buried alive, her husband "grabbed her by the hair, dragged her away, beat her and put her into the house. . . . He threatened her life and kept her captive."[37] Domestic violence occurred even more frequently than in the active subgroup, although this probably reflects lower reporting rates in the latter rather than lower occurrence rates.

Another important aspect of women in the passive partner-assisted infanticide category is the nonbiological relationship between the partner and the child. This relationship is even more striking in this category than among women in the active partner-assisted category: In the passive category the woman's partner was not the biological parent of her child in even a single case. In at least three of the cases, this fact appeared to be particularly salient in the child's death. For example, paternity appeared to play a large role in the case of Pauline Zile. Mrs. Zile's daughter Christina spent most of her life living with relatives out-of-state. She moved in with her mother, stepfather, and half brothers only three months before her death. She was repeatedly abused by Mr. Zile. There are no reports that Mr. Zile abused his biological sons. Additionally, consider again the case of Urbelina Emiliano. Her husband killed her baby because of the shame he believed he would feel if he raised a child that was not biologically his own.

As with women in the active partner-involved category, the majority of women in the passive category had children who were beaten to death. These deaths were also probably the result of extreme discipline. Interestingly, however, two of the children were reported to have been almost constantly beaten and humiliated. It is not clear whether each incident was an attempt at punishment. Some of the incidents seemed to be provoked by rage and hatred toward the child, rather than the result of frustrating toileting incidents, for example.

It is likely that the men's jealousy toward their nonbiological child was a salient factor in the children's death. The fact that all the men in this category were biologically unrelated to the children could explain the high occurrence of continual beatings and humiliations in this category. It is clear that violence directed toward the women and the women's subsequent fear were major contributors to their inability to prevent their children's death.

Other similarities between women in the passive partner-involved category and women in the active category are social context and age of the child. Women in the passive category were also experiencing multiple social stressors such as financial difficulties and cultural isolation. Children in this sample were quite young. They were an average of 33.25 months old.

In sum, women in the passive partner-involved category are similar to those in the active partner-involved category in several ways: they are involved with older, abusive men who are biologically unrelated to their children, they are dealing with multiple social stressors, and their children are quite young and often beaten to death. However, women in the passive partner-involved category have several important distinctions: they are younger than women in the active category, they do not take an active role in the child's death, and, at least in some cases, their partners seem to have tremendous rage and hatred toward their children.

In the next sections we describe the criminal justice system's reaction to these cases of maternal filicide as well as related policy issues.

Analysis

Criminal Justice System's Response

One has only to look at the conviction and sentencing data for women from the partner-involved category to see the criminal justice system's bias against women and lack of understanding about the nature of domestic violence. This bias is most striking in cases from the passive partner-assisted category, because they involve women who did not abuse their children. Rather, the women were held responsible for their child's death because they were expected to be able to prevent their partner from killing their child. Two of the seven women in this sample were not even present when their child was killed, yet were still blamed for not preventing the death. For example, Ivy Lynn Martin, who was not home at the time of her son's murder, received twenty-five years to life for murder, as well as a four-year concurrent term for child endangerment.

The literature suggests that it is not unusual for women who fit into the passive category to be harshly convicted and sentenced, even when they were not present when the crime was committed. The Illinois Supreme Court upheld murder convictions for two women whose boyfriends killed their children, charging that because the women allowed the abuse to occur they were responsible for the deaths. The women were not accused of delivering the abuse themselves. Defense attorneys stated that the women were not aware of the abuse, pointing out that Barbara Peters was not present when her child was killed and that Violetta Burgos did not see signs of abuse because she is legally blind. Peters received thirty years in prison and Burgos received sixty.[38]

In other passive partner-involved cases, women report attempting to stop their partner from murdering their child. In spite of these circumstances, two women were convicted of first-degree murder, one was convicted of second-degree murder, and another was convicted of involuntary manlaughter and child endangerment.

Moral and Legal Blameworthiness

Women's advocates argue that women are held responsible when someone else abuses or kills their child because of society's unrealistic expectations of women, particularly with regard to their mothering role. Consider, for example, several societal expectations of mothers: Mothers are to be married, should primarily or solely work inside the home, should be patient, caring, and nurturing, and should derive intrinsic pleasure from the tasks of cooking, cleaning, and raising children. Society links a woman's self-worth with her ability to fulfill these expectations. When women are unable to live up to these (and countless other) unrealistic expectations, they often feel guilty and ashamed. They believe that other women are able to live up to them and blame themselves for not being good enough.[39]

In truth, the majority of mothers in this country are unmarried, most work outside the home, few, if any, are patient, caring, and nurturing all the time, and many find housecleaning and other such chores tedious and monotonous. However, the media, the justice system, and other aspects of society continue to perpetuate myths about motherhood. Women seldom receive any validation for their natural feelings of boredom, frustration, and impatience. Therefore, they feel deviant when they have such feelings and frequently keep their sentiments to themselves in an effort to prevent others from seeing what "bad" mothers they really are. Depression, isolation, and helplessness may result.[40]

Because of society's unrealistic expectations of women, the occurrence of maternal filicide is viewed with disbelief. In a prior publication, Michelle Oberman stated that maternal filicide is seen as "isolated, and disconnected from—rather than consistent with—what we know about human society" because we are so "mystefied" and "horrified" by the idea of women killing their children. Oberman states that in order to understand maternal filicide we have to put ourselves in these women's shoes and think about the societal expectations they are shouldering.[41]

When we consider the pressures women are faced with, and the guilt and shame they experience when their lives do not match societal expectations, it is not surprising that many women do not ask for help when they need it. Further, even when women do ask for help, services are often not available. After all, when maternal filicide is considered to be an isolated phenomenon, there is no reason to establish services to prevent its occurrence.

The justice system has little sympathy for women who are involved with violent partners. No theory has been consistently accepted in court which explains the connection between a woman's abuse and her ability to protect her children. Rather, consistent with society's tendency to blame these women, the courts view them as passive observers with not enough love for their children to prevent the abuse. As discussed earlier in the chapter, there are numerous reasons why a woman may be unable to leave a violent man or prevent abuse. The justice system completely discounts the woman's own abuse and the harm that may occur to her if she were to leave or attempt to prevent the abuse. In fact, according to law, parents have a duty to protect their children, but are not required to "risk death or serious bodily injury."[42] However, women are held responsible for their children's deaths even though intervention may well result in their own death.

Fathers are not held responsible in the same way. For example, David Schwarz was the father of a child who was killed during the same period of time, in a nearby community, as Christina Zile. Mr. Schwarz's wife, the stepmother of his son, was charged with abusing the boy over an eighteen-month period and eventually killing him. Failure to protect charges were not brought against Mr. Schwarz and the public did not condemn his actions. Instead, Mr. Schwarz was allowed to "get on with his life," while Pauline Zile will spend the rest of her life in prison for her husband's murder of her daughter.[43]

Not only does the justice system have different standards for men and women, but women's efforts to protect their children from violence are often ignored. Many women in partner-involved cases were not the passive observers the courts considered them to be. As previously mentioned, women may stay in a relationship because they have reason to believe, often correctly, that leaving would put their children at even greater risk of harm.[44] Rather than acting as passive observers, many women have made a conscious choice to remain in the relationship because it appeared safer than leaving. Other women are justifiably concerned that if they were to leave the man, he would gain custody or private visitations with their children.[45] These women often remain in a relationship because they are better able to monitor their partners' behavior toward their children by doing so.

In sum, the justice system has different expectations for men and women. Although fathers and mothers legally have the same duty to protect their children, gender role expectations lead to higher standards for women with regard to the care and protection of children. The courts expect women to have a moral obligation to protect their children at all costs, despite laws that specify that parents are not required to protect children at their own expense. The courts clearly separate the best interests of abused children from the best interests of their battered mothers. In this arena, as in all others, women are expected to be completely self-sacrificing. A woman who is unable to protect her child is accused of assigning a higher priority to her relationship than to her duty to protect her child.[46] As we have discussed throughout this chapter, the decision to leave is often an impossible one for battered women.

Policy Implications

Given our knowledge of the complex nature of domestic violence, it is time for the public, as well as the justice system, to reconsider whether it makes sense to blame and punish battered women. If it is truly the justice system's purpose to protect children, as it is often claimed to be, its results have been poor. Punishing battered women has not, and will not, increase the safety of children. The protection of children will increase only when the way in which domestic violence is considered is reframed. Partner-assisted maternal filicide must be considered within a context of domestic violence and the interests of women and children must be considered one and the same.

Perhaps the most important step in preventing the tragedy of maternal filicide, then, is a change in societal attitudes toward women. We must understand the pressures women face and work to debunk the myths of motherhood. We must stop perceiving examples of maternal filicide as isolated events. Our efforts may make it less shameful for women to ask for help and may lead to the development of more services for mothers.

Some progressive thinkers have already recognized that it is too simplistic to discount women who kill their children as bad mothers. They recognize that in doing so, larger cultural and societal influences are ignored. They see that in order to successfully address the problem of maternal filicide, cultural values must shift, thereby encouraging the growth of services for mothers and increasing women's trust and willingness to ask for support. Some professionals are beginning to take a preventive approach by working to recognize risk factors such as the presence of multiple social stressors. A few have even created prevention programs based on these risk factors.

However, one risk factor that has received little attention is the presence of a woman's partner. Although child protective workers and even physicians may be trained to recognize that factors such as a woman's age, economic situation, and substance use may put her child at risk, few recognize that the presence of an abusive partner can be an even larger risk factor. Data from the sample used in this chapter indicate that risk factors include the presence of a male partner who is significantly older than the woman, who is violent toward the woman, and who is not biologically related to the woman's child.

Professionals should be made aware of these risk factors and should be educated about the nature of domestic violence in general. Social service workers, for example, should be aware of the relationship between the woman and her partner and should recognize that the occurrence of domestic violence places the child at risk. Training about the dynamics of domestic violence is imperative. Such training would allow social service workers to recognize that merely telling a woman to leave her abusive partner is not sufficient and may be counterproductive. Forcing her to take parenting classes may not be helpful either. Until women are able to examine and process their violent relationships, they are unlikely to be able to make use of information learned in parenting classes. Women involved in domestically violent relationships may need support and counseling about the nature of domestic violence before they are able to make decisions that are safe for themselves and their children.

Physicians must also be made aware of the risk that a violent partner poses for children in the family. Because women and their children are likely to visit a physician, even if infrequently, health providers may be one of the most important groups we can target with this information. Teachers and day care providers are other groups of people who have frequent contact with mothers and their children.

Of course, having this information is useless unless professionals are able to offer support and guidance in an open-minded, nonthreatening way. As previously discussed, this society has many negative feelings toward women who have abusive partners, often blaming them for staying in the relationship or even for the abuse itself. Professionals as well as the rest of the community need to be better educated about domestic violence so that they are able to provide assistance rather than condemning women in need.

Two Florida counties have designed programs predicated upon the evidence that having a new caretaker in the home is a tremendous risk for young children, particularly those from families that already have the stressors of poverty, neglect, and poor parenting skills. Specifically, in Pinellas and Pasco counties, the Department of Children and Families is sponsoring a new project, the Paramour Intervention Program, which offers intensive counseling, training, and skill-building for new partners. The first step involves a home visit in which counselors observe how the parent and the new partner interact with the children. Counselors then tailor a case plan to their particular needs. Goals include teaching parents nonviolent means of disciplining a child, tools for building a relationship with the child, and skills for permitting the new member to more easily become integrated into the family.[47]

Innovative programs such as this one offer hope that partner-assisted maternal filicides can be prevented. On the other hand, they present the potential for selection bias in favor of monitoring those families that have already come under the scrutiny of state agencies for other reasons. As such, these programs may disproportionately single out poor families and families of color.

Clearly, this chapter illustrates that the complex problem of partner-involved filicide cannot be solved by merely blaming and punishing women. Rather, professionals and community members must work together to build resources to address the larger problem of domestic violence, in addition to working to reduce the isolation of mothers and children who are vulnerable to such violence.

7

RESPONDING TO MOTHERS WHO KILL

Toward a Comprehensive Rethinking of Law, Policy, and Intervention Strategies

❑

When we set out to write this book, we were motivated by the goal of making sense of the "unthinkable" act of a mother killing her own child. In an effort to come to terms with the persistence of this crime, we have approached each case of infanticide asking, "Why did she do it?"

Various commentators have struggled to answer this very question. Their answers often seem to assume that infanticide is an unusual crime, committed by either a very crazy or a very evil woman. For example, Linda Chavez, president of a Washington-based think tank and director of public liaison under President Reagan, refers to women who commit infanticide as "monster-women," and suggests that welfare policy may be linked to infanticide.[1] Indeed, she approves of a statement by Newt Gingrich, who commented upon a particularly gruesome case of murder by asserting, "Welfare policy has created 'a drug addicted underclass with no sense of humanity, no sense of civilization and no sense of the rules of life.'"[2] One psychiatrist, Park Elliot Dietz, offers a theory based upon madness, arguing, "No amount of stress alone can account for women killing their children. . . . It doesn't come from who you hang out with, what your opportunities in life are or how much money you have. It comes from something being wrong with the person."[3]

Our findings, drawn from over two hundred cases of contemporary U.S. infanticide, dispel the notion prevalent in media accounts that infanticide is an isolated crime or a freak occurrence, committed exclusively by women who are either insane or evil. Instead, we have delineated five distinct patterns in contemporary U.S. cases, each of which illustrates a different variation on the same theme: As throughout history, infanticide in the twentieth and twenty-first centuries must be understood as a response to the societal construction of and constraints upon mothering.

Consider briefly each of the five categories of infanticide as they relate to the backdrop of society's expectations of mothers. Although each category reflects distinct patterns of behavior, such that the mothers may have been motivated by different immediate goals and may have used different methods for achieving their goals, there is a profound commonality that links all the infanticide cases. In a sense these categories may be seen as variations on a theme.

Both historically and today, neonaticide may be seen as a "mothering" decision. Typically, these cases involve young pregnant women, who determine, correctly or not, that they would be completely cut off from their social support network were they to disclose their pregnancies. More importantly, they are convinced that they would be exiled from their families, their homes, and their communities were they to attempt to parent their child alone. The terrifying thought of parenting with no money, limited education, few job options, and no one to love and care for them, surely contributes to the panic and denial of pregnancy typically manifested by this population.

Women involved in the assisted-coerced killings of their children are motivated by surprisingly similar fears. These women tend to prioritize their present relationship with a partner over their obligations to protect their children. Often, they themselves are caught in the cycle of an abusive relationship, and are unable to act to protect themselves or their children. They fear that life alone, as a mother with children, would be too difficult, and that they would be bereft without any support system.

Now consider the neglect-related cases of infanticide. These predominantly involve mothers who are parenting under precisely the same conditions feared by the foregoing women. Alone and impoverished, these women make good or adequate parents for the vast majority of the hours and days they spend parenting. On rare occasions, however, they make bad parenting decisions, and some of these decisions have devastating consequences.

What is remarkable about these cases is their gendered nature. These mothers' babies die when they are taking care of other tasks, which are frequently also related to parenting (e.g., a baby is left in the care of an older sibling while the mother is in the kitchen cooking and arguing on the phone with the children's father about finances). To the extent that the deaths occur when the mother is socializing, society is particularly harsh in judging her. Mothering is more than a full-time job. According to the unwritten rules governing the role of motherhood, it is an all-encompassing life change, demanding complete self-abnegation and constant vigilance.

Both the remaining categories of infanticide—those growing out of mental illness, and those that are abuse-related—depict the devastating results of a system that relies on a single individual to parent under these unwritten rules. Whereas women who have strong coping skills and rich social support networks can adapt to society's demands, using friends and family to provide them with relief and companionship, there are some women who find themselves incapable of parenting under these conditions. This is most readily observed in cases involving temporary mental illness, whether depression or psychosis, that renders the woman unable to generate the continual flow of compassion and patience that children demand. Likewise, chronic mental impairment may cause the woman to be constitutionally incapable of meeting the demands of parenting in isolation, without external support.

It is also true that women who kill their children in abuse-related infanticides are affected by the extraordinarily demanding tasks associated with child care. Epidemiologists have demonstrated the specific hours during each day when children are most at risk of death by homicide.[4] They coincide with mealtimes and bedtimes; events that are often accompanied by stress, arguments, and the need to discipline children even in stable, loving households.[5] Seen from this angle, many of the abuse-related cases seem to involve mothers who lacked the impulse-control of their peers. But the impulse that motivated these killings is surprisingly commonplace.

The tasks associated with caring for an infant are extraordinarily demanding. When performed by one parent, twenty-four hours a day, seven days a week, throughout the early months and years of a child's life, this work is arguably the most difficult labor any human ever engages in. The point here is not that infanticide is excusable, but rather that it is far from "unthinkable." Indeed, seen against the backdrop of the construction of motherhood, on rare occasions it may be all but inevitable. The task for a civilized and compassionate society, then, is to determine how to respond to those who kill their children, and more importantly, how to prevent these deaths.

Developing Effective Legal Responses to Infanticide

As noted elsewhere in this book, many countries around the world have recognized the unique circumstances surrounding infanticide and have laws in place that prescribe a consistent and somewhat more lenient treatment for those convicted of this crime. Most noteworthy is the British Infanticide Act, which applies to all women who kill their children within the first twelve months of life. This law is premised upon the belief that a woman who commits infanticide may have done so because "the balance of her mind [i]s disturbed by reason of her not having fully recovered from the effect of giving birth to the child."[6]

According to British scholars, the effect of this statute, in force since 1922, has been "the virtual abandonment of prison sentences as a means of dealing with [this] crime."[7] Although the quasi-scientific basis of this law has been widely criticized, few have questioned the wisdom of its lenience.[8]

Because there are no federal or state statutes governing infanticide in the United States, women who commit similar offenses are tried and sentenced in wildly disparate ways, depending on the predilections of local prosecutors, judges, and juries. For instance, consider the case of Ms. Deborah Gindorf. In 1985, Ms. Gindorf received a life sentence after killing her two young children in a failed homicide-suicide attempt.[9] After attempting to kill herself by several means, she turned herself in to the local police. Doctors evaluating her both for the state and for the defense agreed that she manifested symptoms of psychosis— audio hallucinations and disorganized thinking. But her defense lawyer did not raise the issue of postpartum psychosis at her trial, because there was, at that point in time, very little research to support this phenomenon. In subsequent years, numerous women with symptoms of postpartum psychosis have received little or no jail time for similar crimes.[10] Indeed, even women who lack a diagnosable mental disorder, such as Susan Smith, have been treated far more leniently.[11]

Political considerations may play a particularly noxious role in these cases. For instance, a conservative Illinois state's attorney with statewide political aspirations is seeking the death penalty against Marilyn Lemak, a woman who killed her three young children in a failed attempt at suicide-homicide.[12] Lemak was hospitalized for depression following the birth of her youngest child, and her depression did not abate, but intensified due to the break up of her marriage. History shows that infanticide cases such as this are exceedingly unlikely candidates for the death penalty. This is particularly true in Illinois, where the current governor has placed a moratorium on the death penalty due to widespread evidence of incompetence and unfairness in its administration.[13]

Even more insidious factors such as race appear to have an impact on the administration of justice in infanticide cases. For example, consider the following events from Montgomery County, Ohio. First, in February 1994, Tanisha Nobles, a twenty-one-year-old African-American, was convicted of murder and abuse of a corpse in the drowning death of her two-year-old son.[14] Prior to her arrest, Nobles told the police several false stories about her son's whereabouts, including reporting that her son was kidnaped from a shopping mall. Finally, she told police that she had drowned her son because he had been "getting on her nerves."[15] She was sentenced to fifteen years for the crime.

Six months later, in the same county, seventeen-year-old Rebecca Hopfer, a white girl who lived with her family in a middle-class community, was charged with concealing her pregnancy and murdering her newborn child. At the time of Hopfer's trial, the local press was filled with speculation about how the case should be handled, particularly as the crime related to that committed by Nobles.[16]

Even before the start of Hopfer's trial, the public expressed concern over the potential for racism in handling the case. Despite the major factual differences in the cases, including Hopfer's relative youthfulness and the fact that she readily confessed her crime to the police, both the prosecutor and the community seemed convinced that these cases were sufficiently similar that they should be treated alike.[17] As a result, despite the fact that the county's standard practice was to try all offenders under age eighteen in juvenile court, the county prosecutor made a powerful plea for trying Hopfer as an adult. The judge agreed, and Hopfer was bound over for trial as an adult.[18] Once it was clear that she was to be tried as an adult, the community's sympathies seemed to change, and Hopfer was released on bond.[19] This in turn set loose a barrage of letters to the media, many of which charged that she had received preferential treatment because she was white.[20] This climate continued throughout the trial, ending in a conviction and an identical fifteen-year sentence for Ms. Hopfer.[21]

Although we have argued throughout this book that there are profound similarities linking the many contemporary U.S. infanticide cases, it is patently unjust for the criminal justice system to treat all infanticide cases identically. After all, we lack a statute such as England's, that treats infanticide cases alike on the basis of an explicit justification for mitigating the severity of the punishment for this crime. Thus, each U.S. case should be viewed as involving an individual defendant, whose act arose out of a distinct set of circumstances and whose degree of culpability may therefore vary.

This is not to say that we must embrace the incoherent and arbitrary case law that characterizes U.S. infanticide jurisprudence. Instead, judges and juries should take into consideration factors involving individual blameworthiness. In making their assessment, they should bear in mind that infanticide cases are commonplace, and may be classified according to remarkably consistent patterns, each of which might indicate a distinct degree of culpability. For instance, although both defendants might be deserving of some sympathy, it would be absurd to treat as equivalent the infanticide committed by the mother who suffered from postpartum psychosis and that committed by one who chronically abused her child. Although an articulation of specific legal standards by which these cases should be judged is beyond the scope of this book, it is evident that justice is not served by the randomness with which infanticide cases are presently resolved.[22]

Instead, the criminal justice system must ask what purposes are served by punishing these women. There are three basic justifications for punishment: deterrence, both general and specific, retribution, and rehabilitation. General deterrence refers to the notion that punishment in one case will serve to deter others who contemplate committing the same crime. Given all that we know about the crime of infanticide, it seems highly doubtful at best that the desperate mothers who commit infanticide ever spend time contemplating the potential consequences of their acts. Instead, theirs appears to be a spontaneous crime in virtually all cases, reflecting a loss of control rather than cool-headed calculation.

Specific deterrence refers to the idea that we must punish an individual who has committed a crime in order to deter that individual from committing the same crime again in the future. This argument has some merit when applied to certain categories of infanticide. For instance, one might argue that the mother who kills in an abuse-related infanticide must be punished in order to insure that she understands the limits the law places on disciplining children. Punishment may encourage her to proceed with the utmost caution and support should she ever find herself entrusted with parenting in the future.

On the other hand, it is unlikely that specific deterrence is even relevant to many of the other categories of infanticide. For instance, the woman suffering from either acute or chronic mental illness when she killed her child does not need the law to remind her that her act was heinous. Instead, she needs treatment for her condition, and if it is a temporary one she needs to be assured that she will receive treatment during the early months of caring for any subsequent offspring.

Retribution is predicated upon society's right to punish one who is to blame for the unjustified taking of life. To be sure, we need to cry out against the deaths of these innocent children. And yet, upon examining the patterns that underlie the various categories of infanticide, it often seems difficult to allocate blame to a single individual. Instead, these cases often leave one with the sense that there is blood on more than one pair of hands.

Neonaticide cases, for instance, involve not only the young woman, but also the male who impregnated her, and the family and friends, teachers, and neighbors who never noticed, or who noticed but failed to reach out to assist the pregnant woman. Responsibility also lies with society, which infused all the woman's best options for preventing this outcome—contraception, abortion, adoption, and single parenthood—with a sense of shame and guilt. True, the young woman who bears her child alone, in silent panic, and permits it to drown is not blameless. But it is also clear that others stand to share in some small portion in her blame.

Finally, there is the argument that punishment is necessary for rehabilitative purposes. Given the dismal conditions that prevail in U.S.

prisons, it is difficult for anyone to make the argument that a woman who commits infanticide is likely to be rehabilitated for society by serving time in prison. Indeed, the sort of treatment that these women are likely to need—mental health services, parenting classes, substance abuse treatment—are in particularly scarce supply in women's prisons. These services are much more readily accessible outside prison, and judges can require a woman to obtain any or all of these services as a condition for probation. This solution, probation with counseling, is in essence what the British system requires of women who commit infanticide. Their experience of eighty years with this approach suggests that it is certainly as effective at preventing or deterring infanticide as is incarceration, while being considerably more efficient and cost-effective.[23]

Thus, when considering how the law responds to infanticide, the key question we should ask ourselves is why we are punishing this woman, and what we seek to gain by virtue of her punishment. At times, what we gain may be no more than an opportunity to vent our rage at a life so needlessly lost. At such times, it is imperative to consider the underlying policy factors that have contributed to that lost life.

Developing Effective Policy Responses to Infanticide

History reveals three basic societal postures toward women who kill their children—denial, punishment, or prevention. Denial, or simply ignoring infanticide, seems to have been the most popular approach, as societies throughout history have found it less costly to look the other way when poor women, or even poor families, found themselves unable to cope with the addition of a new baby in their lives.[24]

The punitive approach has also made frequent but brief appearances in recent centuries, supported by those who argue that infanticide, like any other violent crime, must be swiftly and severely punished. Yet societies that have demanded harsh punishment for these defendants find that juries and judges are generally unwilling to comply.

Finally, some societies have adopted policies specifically designed to prevent infanticide. Interestingly, to the extent that these policies have been abandoned, it is due not to their failure, but to the extraordinarily high cost of their success.[25]

In our own era, American public policy may be seen as a combination of denial and punishment. We studiously ignore the frequency of infanticide, and completely fail to observe the underlying similarities or patterns evident in contemporary infanticide cases. Then, when faced with an actual defendant in an infanticide case, we tend to seek the most severe of punishments. Only later, as the judge or jury hears the details of each case, is our anger tempered. And we then cleanse our collective conscience by meting out what we deem to be a just punishment.

If there is one central point to this book, it is this: to the extent that we conceive of the crime of infanticide as a rare and exceptional act committed by a deranged or evil woman, we are dangerously wrong. Indeed, if this society is to have any hope of preventing the deaths of future children at the hands of their mothers, we must begin by changing our tendency to blame only the mothers for this terrible crime. We must begin to identify the myriad ways in which our society tolerates and perpetuates infanticide. And we must take on the work of creating safety nets that are strong enough to catch the mothers who are driven to the edge of despair, permitting us to save both them and their precious children.

NOTES

NOTES TO THE INTRODUCTION

1. William L. Langer, "Infanticide: A Historical Survey," *History of Childhood Quarterly* 1(1974): 353, 355. See also Kathryn L. Moseley, "The History of Infanticide in Western Society," *Issues of Law and Medicine*, 1 (1986): 346–357.

2. Langer, "Infanticide."

3. Langer, "Infanticide." See also Moseley, "History," 346–357.

4. E. A. Wrigley, *Population and History*, 42–43 (New York: McGraw-Hill, 1969). Wrigley notes that anthropologists estimate that Paleolithic parents may have killed as many as 50 percent of their female offspring. Also see Peter C. Hoffer and N. E. H. Hull, *Murdering Mothers: Infanticide in England and New England, 1558–1803* (New York: New York University Press, 1981).

5. Moseley, "History," 346–357.

6. Moseley, "History," 350.

7. Moseley, "History," 349.

8. Moseley, "History," 351.

9. Zainab Chaudhry, "The Myth of Misogyny," *Albany Law Review* 61 (1997): 511, 513.

10. Chaudhry, "Myth."

11. Chaudhry, "Myth."

12. Chaudhry, "Myth."

13. Chaudhry, "Myth."

14. Chaudhry, "Myth," 511, 513.

15. Chaudhry, "Myth," citing the *Qur'an* 4:4. "And give the women (on marriage) their dower as a free gift."

16. Chaudhry, "Myth," 515.

17. Chaudhry, "Myth," citing the *Qur'an* 16:58–59. "When the news is

brought to one of them, of (the birth of) a female (child), his face darkens, and he is filled with inward grief! . . . Shall he retain it . . . or bury it in the dust? Ah! What an evil (choice) they decide on?"

18. Anshu Nangia, "The Tragedy of Bride Burning in India," *Brooklyn Journal of International Law* 22 (1997): 637, 641.

19. Nangia, "Tragedy," 642.

20. Nangia, "Tragedy," 644.

21. Elisabeth Bumiller vividly describes the persistence of female infanticide in contemporary India in her book, *May You Be the Mother of a Hundred Sons* (New York: Ballantine Books, 1990), 104–124.

22. Janice A. Lee, "Family Law of the Two Chinas" *Cardozo Journal of International Comparative Law* 5 (1997): 221.

23. Lee, "Family Law."

24. Lee, "Family Law," 223.

25. Lee, "Family Law," 221.

26. "6.3 Brides for Seven Brothers," *Economist*, December 19, 1998, citing James Z. Lee, *One Quarter of Humanity: Malthusian Mythology and Chinese Realities, 1700–2000* (Cambridge: Harvard University Press, 1999).

Historian William Langer notes that "in ancient times, at least, infanticide was not a legal obligation. It was a practice freely discussed and generally condoned by those in authority and ordinarily left to the decision of the father as the responsible head of the family." Langer, "Infanticide," 353, 355. See also Moseley, "History," 346–351.

Although it is difficult to estimate how widespread infanticide was, historians have documented its persistence through a variety of genres. Demographic studies relying on civil, church, and hospital records yield information about sex-selective infanticidal practices as well as the widespread incidence of infanticide. See Barbara A. Kellum, "Infanticide in England in the Later Middle Ages," *History of Childhood Quarterly* 1 (1974): 368–369; Richard Trexler, "Infanticide in Florence: New Sources and First Results," *History of Childhood Quarterly* 1(1973): 100–102.

27. "6.3 Brides."

28. Susan Greenhalgh and Jiali Li, "Engendering Reproductive Policy and Practice in Peasant China: For a Feminist Demography of Reproduction," *Signs: Journal of Women in Culture and Society* 10 (Spring 1995): 601, 614.

29. Greenhalgh and Li, "Reproductive Policy," 615.

30. Lee, "Family Law," 221.

31. Greenhalgh and Li, "Reproductive Policy," 601.

32. Greenhalgh and Li, "Reproductive Policy."

33. Penelope Mathew, "Case Note: Applicant A v. Minister for Immigration and Ethnic Affairs: The High Court and 'Particular Social Groups': Lessons for the Future," *Melbourne University Law Review* 21(1997): 279.

34. Langer, "Infanticide," 353, 355. See also Moseley, "History," 353–354.

35. Kellum, "Infanticide," 368–369.

36. Kellum, "Infanticide," 368.

37. Kellum, "Infanticide," 369.

38. Moseley, "History," 353–354.

39. Nicholas D. Kristof, "A Mystery from China's Census: Where Have Young Girls Gone," *New York Times,* June 17, 1991.

40. Trexler, "Infanticide in Florence," 98, 100–102 (1973); Kellum, "Infanticide," 368–369.

41. Trexler, "Infanticide in Florence," 101–102; Kellum, "Infanticide," 368–369.

42. Trexler, "Infanticide in Florence," 100–101. Note that modern demographers utilize the same reasoning to document the extent of sex-selective infanticide in modern China and India. Kristof, "Mystery"; Michael Weisskopf, "China's Birth Control Policy Drives Some to Kill Baby Girls," *Washington Post,* January 8, 1985; Thomas Poffenberger, "Child Rearing and Social Structure in Rural India: Toward a Cross-Cultural Definition of Child Abuse and Neglect," in *Child Abuse and Neglect: Cross-Cultural Perspectives,* ed. Jill E. Korbin (Denver: C. Henry Kempe National Center for the Prevention and Treatment of Child Abuse and Neglect, 1981), 71, 78–79. There are 100 boys for every 87 girls in 1971 in Punjab (Poffenberger, "Child Rearing"), and 111.3 boys for every 100 girls in 1990 in China (Kristof, "Mystery").

43. Discrimination against nonmarital children stems from the Bible, which decrees that "A bastard shall not enter the congregation of the Lord; even to his tenth generation shall he not enter the congregation of the Lord." (Deuteronomy 23:2)

44. Susan E. Satava, "Discrimination against the Unacknowledged Illegitimate Child and the Wrongful Death Statute," *Capital University Law Review* 25 (1996): 936, quoting Harry Krause, "Equal Protection for the Illegitimate," *Michigan Law Review* 65 (1967): 477. The common law doctrine of "filius nullius" (literally, "child of no one") establishes the diminished legal status of nonmarital children.

45. Satava, "Discrimination," 937. See also Cindy Bouillon-Jenson, "Infants: History of Infanticide," *Encyclopedia of Bioethics* 3 (1995): 1202.

46.

In 1764, Count Cesare Beccaria, founder of the Classical School of Penal Law, argued in favor of diminishing punishments for justifiable homicides. The key example used to illustrate his argument is that of a single woman who kills her illegitimate newborn baby in an effort to conceal her premarital sexual activity from an intolerant society. Having to choose between ostracism for her and her baby and the death of a being unable to feel the loss of its own life, he asserts that a desperate woman could feel pressed to kill the newborn. According to Beccaria, the killing of a newborn under such special conditions should not be considered a heinous crime but a culpable yet understandable act, deserving a lighter punishment than other circumstances for murder.

Mauro V. Mendlowicz, Mark H. Rapaport, Katia Mecler, Shahrokh Golshan, and Talvane M. Moraes, "A Case-Control Study on the Socio-Demographic Characteristics of 52 Neonaticidal Mothers," *International Journal of Law and Psychiatry* 52 (1998): 209–219, 210 cited.

47. Langer, "Infanticide," 355, 357; Hoffer and Hull, *Murdering Mothers,* 12–13.

48. Hoffer and Hull, *Murdering Mothers,* 13.

49. R. Kellett, "Infanticide and Child Destruction—The Historical, Legal and Pathological Aspects," *Forensic Science International* 53 (1992): 1–28.

50. An Act to Prevent the Destroying and Murthering of Bastard Children, 1623, 21 James I, c. 27, (Eng.).

51. Moseley, "History," 357.

52. Moseley, "History," 356.

53. Trexler, "Infanticide in Florence," 105.

54. Mendlowicz et al., "Case-Control Study," 211.

55. The full text of the law reads as follows:

Where a woman causes the death of her child under twelve months of age, but at the time of the act or omission the balance of her mind was disturbed by reason of her not having fully recovered from the effect of lactation consequent upon the birth of the child, then, notwithstanding that the circumstances were such that but for the Act the offence would have amounted to murder, she shall be guilty of felony, to wit of infanticide, and may for such offence be dealt with and punished as if she had been guilty of the offence of manslaughter of the child.

1938 1 and 2 Geo. VII, c. 36 (Eng.). The 1922 Act was originally limited to "newly born" children, but was amended in 1938 in response to a case that held that the law did not extend to a woman who killed her thirty-five-day-old child. The amended law included any child under the age of twelve months, and extended the defense of lactation-related hormonal imbalance.

56. Michelle Oberman, "Mothers Who Kill: Coming to Terms with Modern American Infanticide," *American Criminal Law Review* 34 (1996): 17. Additionally, the legal standards of proof regarding the mental status of women accused of infanticide are looser than the modern insanity defense, and thus this defense is available to virtually all women accused of killing their young children. For example, one study of eighty-nine British women who killed their children between 1970 and 1975 demonstrated the efficiency of the infanticide statute, as compared with other homicide laws, in obtaining convictions. Sixty subjects were charged with murder, as their victims exceeded the age of one year, yet only two were convicted of this offense. P. T. d'Orban, "Women Who Kill Their Children," *British Journal of Psychiatry* 134 (1979): 566–567. The vast majority of these defendants were convicted of manslaughter on grounds of diminished responsibility or lack of intent to kill. d'Orban, "Women Who Kill." Five were acquitted altogether. In contrast, of 24 subjects charged with infanticide, 23 were convicted. Of the 23 convicted, 18 received probationary sentences (7 on condition that they receive psychiatric treatment), 2 were sentenced to imprisonment (one for eighteen months and the other for two and a half years), 1 was conditionally charged, 1 received a nominal one-day sentence, and another was diagnosed as suffering from postpartum depression and admitted to a mental hospital. d'Orban, "Women Who Kill."

57. Indeed, the most recent edition of the American Psychiatric Association's *Diagnostic and Statistical Manual of Mental Disorders* (4th ed. 1994) refuses to list postpartum psychosis as a distinct psychiatric ailment. Instead, it treats classifies postpartum ailments according to their general variety of mental illness, and simply qualifies the diagnosis by noting the timing of onset as "postpartum." *American Psychiatric Association, Diagnostic and Statistical Manual of Mental Disorders,* 4th ed. (Washington, D.C.: American Psychiatric Association, 1994).

58. Michael W. O'Hara, "Postpartum 'Blues,' Depression and Psychosis: A Review," *Journal of Psychosomatice Obstetrics and Gynecology* 7 (1987): 205.

59. Mary E. Lentz, "A Postmortem of the Postpartum Psychosis Defense," *Capital University Law Review* 18 (1989): 532. Some report a belief that the child is a phantom, or was "conceived from unnatural processes such as impregnation by the devil."

60. d'Orban, "Women Who Kill," 567; O'Hara "Postpartum 'Blues,'" 220.

61. Eric Lichtblau, "Appeal Argued in Postpartum Case," *Los Angeles Times,* May 24, 1990.

62. Lichtblau, "Appeal Argued."

63. O'Hara "Postpartum 'Blues,'" 217–218.

64. Larry King, "Larry King Live: A Mother Tells Why She Killed Her Son" (CNN television broadcast, November 17, 1994), interviewing Milton Grimes, criminal defense attorney for Sheryl Massip.

65. One brief study attempts to prove this by using statistics gathered from the National Center on Vital Statistics. David Lester, "Roe v. Wade Was Followed by a Decrease in Neonatal Homicide" *Journal of the American Medical Association,* 267(1992): 3027. Of course it is important to remember that legalizing abortion does not guarantee access to abortion.

66. See www.census.gov/population/socdemo/ms-la/tabch-1.txt.

67. See Rosemary Gartner, "Family Structure, Welfare Spending, and the Child Homicide in Developed Democracies," *Journal of Marriage and the Family* 53 (February 1991): 231–240, for a discussion of the relationship between family structure and infanticide. The geographical structure of American communities reinforces a sense of isolation. Author James Kuntsler documents the post–World War II shift away from close-knit towns with cen-

tralized gathering places to atomized suburbs and cities, in which inhabitants must use cars to procure goods from stores located in stripmalls. See James H. Kuntsler, *The Geography of Nowhere: The Rise and Decline of America's Man-Made Landscape* (New York: Simon and Schuster, 1993).

68. There is a growing literature exploring the tendency of survivors of abusive childhoods to replicate abusive family patterns as adults. For a summary of this literature, see U.S. Advisory Board on Child Abuse and Neglect, *A Nation's Shame: Fatal Child Abuse and Neglect in the United States,* 5th Report (1995), 7. This study found that "the average abusive parent is in his or her mid-twenties, lives near or below the poverty level, often has not finished high school, is depressed and unable to cope with stress, and has experienced violence first hand." *Fatal Child Abuse,* 71.

69. *Fatal Child Abuse,* 71. See Nora Dougherty, "The Holding Environment: Breaking the Cycle of Abuse," *Soc. Casework* 64 (1983): 283; Brandt Steele, "Reflections on the Therapy for Those Who Maltreat Children," in *The Battered Child,* ed. Ray E. Helfer and Ruth S. Kempe (Chicago: University of Chicago Press, 1998), 382–391; Susan L. Smith, "Significant Research Findings in the Etiology of Child Abuse," *Soc. Casework* 65 (1984): 344.

70. See Sally Cantor, "Inpatient Treatment of Adolescent Survivors of Sexual Abuse," in *Child Survivors and Perpetrators of Sexual Abuse: Treatment Innovations,* ed., Mic Hunter (1995), 24. William N. Friedrich, "Managing Disorders of Self-Regulation in Sexually Abused Boys," in *Child Survivors and Perpetrators of Sexual Abuse,* 3; Ruth S. Kempe, "A Developmental Approach to the Treatment of an Abused Child," in *The Battered Child,* 360–381; Elizabeth A. W. Seagull, "The Child Psychologist's Role in Family Assessment," in *The Battered Child,* 152–177.

71. Studies have noted a correlation between child abuse fatalities and household isolation, whether in rural or urban areas. Not only is abusive behavior more likely to occur when the primary caretaker receives no parenting support from neighbors, friends, and relatives, but it is less likely to be discerned and thereby prevented by others. *Fatal Child Abuse,* 125–126, citing National Research Council, *Understanding Child Abuse and Neglect* (Washington D.C.: National Academy Press, 1993)). See also Smith, "Significant Research Findings," 338.

72. Anthony B. Klapper, "Finding a Right in State Constitutions for

Community Treatment of the Mentally Ill," *University of Pennsylvania Law Review* 42 (1993): 751.

73. Henry J. Steadman et al., "Criminology: The Impact of State Mental Hospital Deinstitutionalizations on United States Prison Population, 1968–1978," *Criminal Law and Criminology* 75 (1984): 475, citing Howard H. Goldman, Neal H. Adams, and Carl A. Taube, "Deinstitutionalization: The Data Demythologized," *Hospital Community Psychiatry* 34 (1983): 129.

74. Steadman, "Criminology."

75. Steadman, "Criminology," 478.

76. Klapper, "Finding," 739, 750, 752, the last citing Samuel J. Brakel et al., *The Mentally Disabled and the Law* (Chicago: University of Chicago Press, 1985).

77. Klapper, "Finding."

78. Klapper, "Finding," 753.

79. Klapper, "Finding," 753, citing Adrianne Carr, *The Scary Situation in Our Shelters, Washington Post,* December 13, 1992, C8.

80. Klapper, "Finding," 753.

81. Klapper, "Finding."

82. Eric Zorn, "For Garcia, Commutation May Be Ultimate Punishment," *Chicago Tribune,* January 17, 1996.

83. Kathryn Kahler, "Women on Death Row: A Chilling Sign of the Times," *Plain Dealer*, May 26, 1993.

84. Laurence Hammack, "Woman Accused of Murder; Seven-Month-Old Son Died in Bathtub," *Roanoke Times,* December 6, 1994.

NOTES TO CHAPTER I

1. Neonaticide was defined by Resnick as the killing of a newborn on the day of its birth or within twenty-four hours of birth. Phillip J. Resnick, "Murder of the Newborn: A Psychiatric Review of Neonaticide," *American Journal of Psychiatry* 126 (April 1970): 1414–1420.

2. Filicide is the act of killing one's own child.

3. There are various theories as to why Susan Smith killed her children. However, prevention and intervention strategies for any of these motivations would inevitably be very different than for Melissa Drexler.

4. Phillip J. Resnick, "Child Murder by Parents: A Psychiatric Review of Filicide," *American Journal of Psychiatry* 126 (September 1969): 325–334. See also Resnick, "Murder of the Newborn."

5. Resnick, "Child Murder by Parents," 325–326.

6. Although spousal revenge, or the Medea Syndrome, has repeatedly been identified as a motive for men there has never been any evidence to support it as a motive for women. Even as recently as 1999, Dube and Hodgins found support for the Medea Syndrome in men but not in women. Myriam Dube and Sheilagh Hodgins, "Retrospective Study of Filicide: Risk Factors and Behavioral Precursors in Cohort of Quebec Parents," paper presented at Victimization of Children and Youth: An International Research Conference, June 2000, Durham, New Hampshire.

7. P. D. Scott, "Parents Who Kill Their Children," *Medicine, Science and the Law* 13 (April 1973): 120–126, citing p. 121.

8. June Baker, "You Can't Let Your Children Cry: Filicide in Victoria 1978–1988," Unpublished M.A. thesis, Criminology Department, University of Melbourne, Victoria, Australia, 1991.

9. Scott, "Parents Who Kill."

10. Resnick, "Murder of the Newborn," 1419.

11. Resnick, "Murder of the Newborn," 1415.

12. For example, the 1994 version of the *Diagnostic and Statistical Manual* introduced a cultural component for psychiatric evaluation. See American Psychiatric Association, *Diagnostic and Statistical Manual of Mental Disorders* 4th ed. (Washington, D.C.: American Psychiatric Association, 1994).

13. Stephen A. Mitchell and Margaret J. Black, *Freud and Beyond* (New York: Basic Books, 1995).

14. Scott, "Parents Who Kill," 121–122. Emphasis in original.

15. Resnick, "Murder of the Newborn," 1415.

16. *Griswold v. Connecticut*, 381 US 479 (1965).

17. *Eisenstadt v. Baird*, 405 US 438 (1972).

18. *Roe v. Wade*, 410 US 113 (1973).

19. Scott, "Parents Who Kill."

20. P. T. d'Orban, "Women Who Kill Their Children," *British Journal of Psychiatry* 134 (1979): 560–571.

21. Baker, "You Can't Let."

22. Dominique Bourget and John Bradford, "Homicidal Parents," *Canadian Journal of Psychiatry* 35 (April 1990): 233–238.

23. Baker, "You Can't Let."

24. Baker, "You Can't Let," 87.

25. These included attempted and successful suicides.

26. Christine M. Alder and June Baker, "Maternal Filicide: More Than One Story to Be Told," *Women and Criminal Justice* 2 (1997): 15–39, citing p. 28.

27. Alder and Baker, "Maternal Filicide," 32.

28. Alder and Baker, "Maternal Filicide," 33.

29. Ania Wilczynski, *Child Homicide* (New York: Oxford University Press, 1997).

30. Wilczynski, *Child Homicide*, 14.

31. Wilczynski, *Child Homicide*, 14.

32. Wilczynski, *Child Homicide*, 15.

33. Wilczynski, *Child Homicide*, 43. Wilczynski also identified eight clusters of risk factors for child homicide. The demographic cluster included age, relationship to victim, gender, class, and ethnicity. Characteristics in the social cluster included child care responsibilities, lack of sleep, marital status, biological parents' marital status at victim's birth, source of income, financial problems, accommodation problems, youthful parenthood, lack of preparation for parenting, education, and criminal convictions. The psychiatric cluster included substance use, prior suicide attempts, and prior symptoms of depression and diagnosis of mental disorder. The fourth cluster, victim characteristics, included number of victims, gender, age, sibling rank, surviving siblings, ethnicity, victim perceived as difficult to care for, victim's behavior seen as a precipitant for killing, and a difficult birth. Characteristics under the situational cluster were location of offense, delay in seeking assistance, notification to authorities, confession by perpetrator, denial by perpetrator, remorse by perpetrator, method of killing, violence toward others at the time of the filicide, and suicidal behavior at the time of the filicide. The fifth cluster reflected prior family conflict and maltreatment and included relationship problems, domestic violence, prior violence toward the victim, other maltreatment, and abuse of siblings. The seventh cluster referred to family history including family criminality, family psychiatric history, and

problems in childhood history. Finally, the last cluster involved prior contact with agencies.

The impact of these clusters, and factors within these clusters, are described in detail by Wilczynski. They are perhaps best summarized by Wilczynski's discussion of the typical child killer:

The present study has identified numerous common risk factors for child homicide, which can aid in both understanding why it occurs and preventing its occurrence. From this analysis it appears that child homicide offenders are characterised by three features, and that there are some important sex differences in the risk factors for this crime. (Child Homocide, *101*)

The risk factors identified in Wilczynski's study highlight three main characteristics of child homicide offenders: they have numerous problems, a negative perception of their situation, and a lack of social and personal resources with which to cope with their difficulties. Wilczynski, *Child Homocide,* 101.

34. One final typology emerged in 1998. Silva, Leong, Dassori, Ferrari, Weinstock, and Yamamoto proposed a multilevel system of classification, which was quite comprehensive and included an evaluation of psychiatric/diagnostic factors, developmental factors, behavioral nonpsychopathological factors, and psychosociocultural/ecological factors. Their system complements the present typology but is meant to be, and is an excellent template for, individual evaluation and treatment planning.

However, the present typology was meant to guide policy, prevention, and intervention strategies rather than assist in individual treatment. Our typology was developed to reflect a multifaceted approach to the problem of maternal filicide. See J. Arturo Silva, Gregory B. Leong, Albana Dassori, Michelle M. Ferrari, Robert Weinstock, and Joe Yamamoto, "A Comprehensive Typology for the Biopsychosociocultural Evaluation of Child-Killing Behavior," *Journal of Forensic Science* 43 (1998): 1112–1118.

35. Michelle Oberman, "Mothers Who Kill: Coming to Terms with Modern American Infanticide," *American Criminal Law Review* (Fall 1996): 1–110, citing pp. 32–33.

36. The first set of terms was "(baby or infant or child! or newborn) w/10 (mother!) w/10 (kill! or murder! or manslaughter or homicide)." An exclamation point finds all derivatives of the root word and "w/10" means that the terms in each parenthesis have to be within ten words of each

other. So this search translated into assessing all cases where a child (or variants) was mentioned in close proximity with mother and homicide (or variants). The second set of terms was "(baby or infant or newborn or child!) w/10 (wom*n or mother! or girl!) w/10 (garbage or trash or bathroom or toilet or dumpster or drown! or suffocat[e]! or smother!)." This search was aimed more at the neonaticide cases and identified most of the common places in which a neonaticidal mother will give birth or dispose of the body. These searches still produced thousands of citations. In all, approximately five hundred of them were relevant cases. It should be noted, however, that this number likely represents a *very* small proportion of the actual cases of filicide as many victims are never found and/or many newspapers do not cover the story.

37. For example, alleged attachment disorder in a child who was not adopted as an infant.

38. A complete listing of all databases searched includes: Bioethicsline, PsycINFO, MEDLINE, Dissertation Abstracts, Social Sciences Citation Index, Science Citation Index, Humanities Citation Index, LEXIS, WorldCat, Bureau of Justice Statistics, A Matter of Fact, National Criminal Justice Referral Service, Index to Legal Periodicals, Anthropological Literature, CINAHL, Contemporary Women's Issues, ERIC, PAIS, Papers 1st, Proceedings 1st, Periodical Abstracts, SIRS, Newspaper Abstracts, and Ethnic Newswatch.

39. Wilczynski, *Child Homicide*, 11.

40. See Wilczynski, *Child Homicide,* and Baker, "You Can't Let," for discussions of previous methods and failures with them.

41. When a story was reported through a newswire such as the Associated Press and several articles in various newspapers resulted, these were not treated as independent reports.

42. Wilczynski, *Child Homicide*, 11.

43. See Scott Kidd, "A Case Study of a Jonesboro, Arkansas School Shooting Offender," and Kathleen M. Heide, Eldra P. Solomon, Cary Hopkins Eyles, and Erin Spencer, "School Shootings in the U.S.: The Portrait of Lethal Violence and the Blueprint for Prevention," both papers presented at the Academy of Criminal Justice Sciences Annual Meeting, March 1997, Orlando, Florida.

44. Wilczynski, *Child Homicide*, 91; Heide et al., "School Shootings"; and Dube and Hodgins, "Retrospective Study of Filicide."

45. See, for example, Alder and Baker, "Maternal Filicide," or Wilczynski, Ch. 10.

46. Cheryl L. Meyer, Tara C. Proano, and James R. Franz, "Postpartum Syndromes: Disparate Treatment in the Legal System," in *It's a Crime: Women and Justice,* ed. Roslyn Muraskin (Upper Saddle River, N.J.: Prentice Hall, 2000.

NOTES TO CHAPTER 2

1. Linda Valdez, "Another Dead Baby Testifies to Consequences of Devalued Sex," *Arizona Republic*, November 14, 1997, B6.

2. Dominique Bourget and Alain Labelle, "Homicide, Infanticide, and Filicide," *Clinical Forensic Psychiatry* 15 (September 1992): 661–673.

3. Phillip J. Resnick, "Child Murder by Parents: A Psychiatric Review of Filicide," *American Journal of Psychiatry* 126 (September 1969): 325–334.

4. M. Brozovsky and H. Falit, "Neonaticide: Clinical and Psychodynamic Considerations," *Journal of the American Academy of Child Psychiatry* 10 (1971): 673–683.

5. Steven Pinker, "Why They Kill Their Newborns," *New York Times,* November 2, 1997, 52.

6. Jackie Leyden, "All Things Considered," National Public Radio, June 27, 1997.

7. David Lester, "The Murder of Babies in American States: Association with Suicide Rates," *Psychological Reports* 71 (December 1992): 1202.

8. Bourget and Labelle, "Homicide, Infanticide, and Filicide," 668.

9. H. Gummersbach, "Die Kriminalpsychologische Personalichkeit der Kindesmorderinn und ihre Wertung im Gerichtesmedizinischen Gutachen," *Wiener Medizinische Wochenschrift* 88 (1938): 1151–1155.

10. Peter Cummings, Mary Fay Theis, Beth A. Mueller, and Frederick Rivara, "Infant Injury and Death in Washington State, 1981 through 1990," *Archives of Pediatric and Adolescent Medicine* 148 (October 1994): 1021–1026.

11. Sara J. Emerick, Laurence R. Foster, and Douglas T. Campbell, "Risk

Factors for Traumatic Infant Death in Oregon, 1973 to 1982," *Pediatrics* 77 (April 1986): 518–522.

12. Mary D. Overpeck, Ruth A. Brenner, Ann C. Trumble, Lara B. Trifiletti, and Heinz W. Berendes, "Risk Factors for Infant Homicide in the United States," *New England Journal of Medicine* 339 (October 1998): 1211–1216.

13. Christine M. Alder and June Baker, "Maternal Filicide: More than One Story to Be Told," *Women and Criminal Justice* 9 (1997): 15–39.

14. Allison Morris and Ania Wilczynski, "Rocking the Cradle: Mothers Who Kill Their Children," in *Moving Targets: Women, Murder, and Representation*, ed. Helen Birch (Berkeley: University of California Press, 1994).

15. Steven E. Pitt and Erin M. Bale, "Neonaticide, Infanticide, and Filicide: A Review of the Literature," *Bulletin of the American Academy of Psychiatry and the Law* 23, no. 3 (1995): 375–386.

16. Alder and Baker, "Maternal Filicide," 30–31.

17. Phillip J. Resnick, "Murder of the Newborn: A Psychiatric Review of Neonaticide," *American Journal of Psychiatry* 126 (April 1970): 1414–1420; Alder and Baker, "Maternal Filicide"; P. T. d'Orban, "Women Who Kill Their Children," *British Journal of Psychiatry* 134 (1979): 560–571.

18. C. Brezinka, O. Huter, W. Biebl, and J. Kinzl, "Denial of Pregnancy: Obstetrical Aspects," *Journal of Psychosomatic Obstetrics and Gynecology* 15 (1994): 1–8.

19. Many authors have talked about the ongoing cultural stigma surrounding births deemed to be illegitimate. They include Edward Saunders, "Neonaticides following 'Secret' Pregnancies: Seven Case Reports," *Public Health Reports* 104 (July–August 1989): 368–372; and Pitt and Bale, "Neonaticide, Infanticide, and Filicide"; Anna M. Spielvogel and Heide C. Hohener, "Denial of Pregnancy: A Review and Case Reports," *Birth Issues in Perinatal Care* 22 (1998): 220–226.

20. C. M. Green and S. V. Manohar, "Neonaticide and Hysterical Denial of Pregnancy," *British Journal of Psychiatry* 156 (1990): 121–123, p.123 cited.

21. Alder and Baker, "Maternal Filicide." Even women who come from economically advantaged families may not themselves have the financial resources or independent access to funds required either to seek out abortions or to subsist as single parents.

22. Martha Smithey, "Infant Homicide: Victim/Offender Relationship and Causes of Death," *Journal of Family Violence* 13 (1998): 285–297.

23. Resnick, "Murder of the Newborn."

24. Overpeck et al., "Risk Factors for Infant Homicide in the United States."

25. Catherine E. Lewis, Madelon V. Baronoski, Josephine A. Buchanan, and Elissa P. Benedak, "Factors Associated with Weapon Use in Maternal Filicide," *Journal of Forensic Science* 43 (1998): 613–618.

26. Smithey, "Infant Homicide."

27. Susan Crimmins, Sandra Langley, Henry H. Brownstein, and Barry J. Spunt, "Convicted Women Who Have Killed Children: A Self-Psychology Perspective," *Journal of Interpersonal Violence* 12 (1997): 49–69.

28. Crimmins, Langley, Brownstein, and Spunt, "Convicted Women," 30–31.

29. J. Arturo Silva, Gregory B. Leong, Albana Dassori, Michelle M. Ferrari, Robert Weinstock, and Joe Yamamoto, "A Comprehensive Typology for the Biopsychosociocultural Evaluation of Child-Killing Behavior," *Journal of Forensic Science* 43 (1998): 1112–1118.

30. Tovia Smith, "All Things Considered," National Public Radio, July 9, 1998.

31. Norma Meyer, "The Garden of Angels: In Death, Discarded Babies Are Adopted by a Stranger," *San Diego Union-Tribune,* July 12, 1998.

32. See case regarding Audrey Iaconna in Steve Luther, "Papers Unsealed in Audrey Case," *Plain Dealer,* February 18, 1998, 1B; and of Typhanie Pleasant in Deborah Yetter, "Woman, 22, on Trial for Murder a Year after Burying Baby in Back Yard," *Courier-Journal,* January 14, 1994, 6B.

33. See case regarding Typhanie Pleasant in Yetter, "Woman, 22."

34. Michelle Oberman, "Mothers Who Kill: Coming to Terms with Modern American Infanticide," *American Criminal Law Review* 24 (Fall 1996): 1–110.

35. Dennis Wagner, "Teen's Secret Brings Tragedy: Smothered Newborn Ends 9-Month Ordeal," *Phoenix Gazette,* February 1, 1995, A1.

36. While Julie's case is slightly less typical than the others, given her age above the mean, other factors were similar. Catherine Lewis has studied older

women who commit neonaticide and believes that other extenuating factors may contribute to their behaviors (e.g., history of physical and/or sexual abuse, substance abuse history, financial hardship as opposed to deep sense of shame, possibly higher rates of psychopathology, and so on). See Carl Sherman, "Older Women Are Also Capable of Committing Neonaticide," *Clinical Psychiatry News* 27 (1999): 22.

37. Alder and Baker, "Maternal Filicide"; Brezinka, Huter, Biebl, and Kinzl, "Denial of Pregnancy"; and Spielvogel and Hohener, "Denial of Pregnancy."

38. Brezinka, Huter, Biebl, and Kinzl, "Denial of Pregnancy"; and Spielvogel and Hohener, "Denial of Pregnancy."

39. Vicky Que, "All Things Considered," National Public Radio, July 9, 1998.

40. Oberman, "Mothers Who Kill."

41. Brezinka, Huter, Biebl, and Kinzl, "Denial of Pregnancy," 1.

42. Green and Manohar, "Neonaticide and Hysterical Denial of Pregnancy."

43. Neil S. Kaye, Online resource: http://www.courtpsychiatrist.com/neonaticide.html.

44. Geoffrey R. McKee and Steven J. Shea, "Maternal Filicide: A Cross-National Comparison," *Journal of Clinical Psychology* 54 (1998): 679–687.

45. This statistic should be interpreted cautiously as the cited study included filicidal parents (both men and women), and not just neonaticidal women.

46. Morris and Wilczynski, "Rocking the Cradle," 215.

47. Catherine Bonnet, "Adoption at Birth: Prevention against Abandonment or Neonaticide," *Child Abuse and Neglect* 17 (1993): 501–513.

48. 1938 1 and 2 Geo. VII, c. 36 (Eng.).

49. However, this should not be taken to suggest that mental illness rates are higher than initially discussed. Instead, it is a call for the analysis of women's cognitive functioning and psychological wherewithal during labor and the subsequent neonaticidal act. See James J. Dvorak, "Neonaticide: Less than Murder," *Northern Illinois University Law Review* 19 (Fall 1998): 173.

50. C. A. Fazio and J. L. Comito, "Rethinking the Tough Sentencing of

Teenage Neonaticide Offenders in the United States," *Fordham Law Review* 67 (May 1999): 3109 and Oberman, "Mothers Who Kill."

51. This decision was later reversed and sent back to circuit court because it was determined that the jury had not been appropriately instructed of an alternative defense, namely, "mistake of fact." See Nikita Stewart, "Woman's Conviction in Death of Baby Reversed," *Courier-Journal,* December 23, 1994, 4B. No media accounts ever reported the final results of Tonya's case. This is not uncommon. Oberman, "Mothers Who Kill," found that of the 47 cases she studied, dispositions were only reported for 15. As for the 37 women included in this study, outcomes are known for only 19. Additionally, Schwartz and Isser included the study of 86 neonaticidal women, only 44 of which were reported with a final disposition. See Lita L. Schwartz and Natalie K. Isser, *Endangered Children: Neonaticide, Infanticide, and Filicide* (Boca Raton, Fla.: CRC Press, 2000).

52. Smith, "All Things Considered."

53. Schwartz and Isser, *Endangered Children.*

54. Beth E. Bookwalter, "Throwing the Bath Water out with the Baby: Wrong for Exclusion of Expert Testimony in Neonaticide Syndrome," *Boston University Law Review* 78 (October 1998): 1185–1210.

55. *People v. Wernick,* 632 NYS 2d 839.

56. In 2000, a case was recently brought forth in Cincinnati, Ohio, in which a twenty-year-old woman was sentenced to life in prison for committing neonaticide after a defense of Neonaticide Syndrome was rejected by the court. See S. Kemme, "Mom Gets Life for Killing Newborn," *Cincinnati Enquirer,* March 24, 2000.

57. Pitt and Bale, "Neonaticide, Infanticide, and Filicide," 380.

58. David Lester, "Roe v. Wade Was Followed by a Decrease in National Neonatal Homicide," *Journal of the American Medical Association* 267 (1992): 3027–3028.

59. David Lester, "Legal Abortions and Neonatal Homicide After Roe v. Wade," *Psychological Reports* 72 (1993): 46.

60. Barbara Ehrenreich, "Where Have All the Babies Gone?" *Life* 21 (1998): 68–76.

61. Gia Fenoglio, "Another Front in the Abortion Wars," *National Journal* 33 (February 10, 2001): 432.

62. Bourget and Labelle, "Homicide, Infanticide, and Filicide."

63. Diana J. Schemo, "Survey Finds Parents Favor More Detailed Sex Education," *New York Times,* October 4, 2000, A1.

64. Robert Kaplan and Therese Grotowski, "Denied Pregnancy," *Australian and New Zealand Journal of Psychiatry* 30 (1996): 861–863.

65. These authors based their recommendation on suggestions already found in the literature. See David H. Strauss, Robert L. Spitzer, and Philip R. Muskin, "Maladaptive Denial of Physical Illness: A Proposal for DSM-IV," *American Journal of Psychiatry* 147 (1990): 1168–1172, and Laura J. Miller, "Maladaptive Denial of Pregnancy," *American Journal of Psychiatry* 148 (1991): 1108.

66. *20/20,* ABC, August 8, 2000. Faris was also profiled in *People Magazine* on January 24, 2000.

67. Such programs were the focus of the February 21, 2000, issue of *Time* magazine. Alabama, Minnesota, and Texas had programs in existence. Texas also has a state law in which criminal penalties cannot be brought toward a person who leaves a child, age thirty days or younger, at a licensed emergency medical facility. See E. Hanson, "Newborn's Body Found in Dumpster; Teen Faces Charges as New Law Begins," *Houston Chronicle,* September 3, 1999: A29. Recent reviews have cited that twelve states have adopted "safe haven" laws and twenty-six additional states have considered such legislation. See Michael S. Raum and Jeffrey L. Skaare, "Encouraging Abandonment: The Trend toward Allowing Parents to Drop off Unwanted Newborns," *North Dakota Law Review* 76 (2000): 49–53.

68. Susan Schindehette, "Last Embrace," *People Magazine,* January 24, 2000, 49–53.

NOTES TO CHAPTER 3

1. Tom Morganthau, "Condemned to Life," *Newsweek*, August 7, 1995.

2. Ania Wilczynski, "Images of Women Who Kill Their Infants: The Mad and the Bad," *Women and Criminal Justice* 2 (1991): 72.

3. Wilczynski, "Images of Women," 78.

4. *Dusky v. United States,* 362 U.S. 402 (1960).

5. 10 Cl. & F. 200, 8 Eng. Rep 718 (H.L. 1843).

6. But the criteria in South Carolina were actually even more stringent.

7. This excludes mental retardation.

8. American Psychiatric Association, *Diagnostic and Statistical Manual of Mental Disorders,* 4th ed. (Washington, D.C.: American Psychiatric Association, 1994), 629.

9. American Psychiatric Association, *Diagnostic and Statistical Manual,* 629.

10. American Psychiatric Association, *Diagnostic and Statistical Manual,* 629.

11. American Psychiatric Association, *Diagnostic and Statistical Manual,* 629.

12. Morganthau, "Condemned to Life."

13. Tony Rizzo, "Green Gets Life Sentence," *Kansas City Star,* May 31, 1996.

14. Rizzo, "Green Gets Life Sentence."

15. J. Steven Dillon, "Mother Details Fatal Assault," *Courier*, February 4, 1997.

16. Jeffrey Susman, "Postpartum Depressive Disorders," *Journal of Family Practice* 43 (1996): S17.

17. Susman, "Postpartum Depressive Disorders," S17–S18.

18. Susman, "Postpartum Depressive Disorders," S18.

19. J. Steven Dillon, "Midwife Testifies Snyder Exhibited Signs of Depression," *Courier*, January 31, 1997.

20. Cheryl L. Meyer, Tara C. Proano, and James R. Franz, "Postpartum Syndromes: Disparate Treatment in the Legal System," in *It's a Crime: Women and Justice,* ed. Roslyn Muraskin (Upper Saddle River, N.J.: Prentice Hall, 2000), 92.

21. J. Steven Dillon, "Testimony Hurts Kim Snyder's Defense: Assault Is Reenacted," *Courier*, February 5, 1997.

22. "Mom Pleads Guilty in Death of Infant," *Dayton Daily News*, July 9, 1998.

23. Laura E. Reece, "Mothers Who Kill: Postpartum Disorders and Criminal Infanticide," *UCLA Law Review* 38 (1991): 706.

24. Mark Henry, "The Reasons Behind This Madness," *Press-Enterprise*, August 5, 1994.

25. Henry, "The Reasons."

26. Frederick Kunkle and Debra Lynn Vial, "Four Shot Dead in Montclair; Firefighters Find Mom, Daughters," *Record* (Bergen County), January 23, 1997.

27. Abby Goodnough, "Investigators in Montclair Focus on Murder-Suicide," *Record* (Bergen County), January 24, 1997.

28. Steve Gutterman, "Woman Charged in Death of 3-Year-Old Son," Associated Press, November 9, 1998.

29. "Judge Calls for 2nd Psychiatric Examination of Mother in Murder Case," Associated Press, January 20, 1999.

30. Tillie Fong, "Mom Gets Maximum Sentence of 48 Years for Drowning Son," *Denver Rocky Mountain News*, February 12, 2000.

31. Faye Fiore, "Mother's Fears End in Tragedy; Suicide: A Woman Who Was Described as Profoundly Depressed Drives Her Van into L.A. Harbor. Her Four Children Die With Her," *Los Angeles Times*, January 24, 1991.

32. Don Baird, "Mother Insane in Killing; Psychiatric Help Slated for Woman Who Killed Child," *Columbus Dispatch*, May 19, 1995.

33. These cases do not include Munchausen's Syndrome by Proxy.

34. Geoffrey Nelson, "Life Strains, Coping, and Emotional Well-Being: A Longitudinal Study of Recently Separated and Married Women," *American Journal of Community Psychology* 17 (1989): 461.

35. Suzanne M. Bianchi and Daphne Spain, "Women, Work, and Family in America," *Population Bulletin* 51 (1996): 12.

36. Sharon Comitz, Glenn Comitz, and Diane M. Semprevivo, "Postpartum Psychosis: A Family's Perspective," *NAACOGS Clinical Issues in Perinatal and Women's Health Nursing* 1 (1990): 416.

37. Rizzo, "Green Gets Life Sentence."

38. It should be noted, however, that personality disorders are a source of some controversy among psychologists. They are renowned for being difficult to diagnose and treat. This is not surprising, given that people with personality disorders often do not perceive themselves to be disordered and are not seeking treatment but are referred. Moreover, it may take a clinician quite a long time before a personality disorder can be detected.

39. We realize that this diagnosis represents speculation on our part but felt it was necessary to convey our hypotheses. There has been tremendous

discussion and debate within the psychological community regarding gender biases in the definition and diagnosis of personality disorders. Central to the controversy is the argument that women are diagnosed for personality disorders when they do not fit social stereotypes for appropriate female behavior. Specifically, women diagnosed with borderline personality disorder may be receiving the diagnosis because they do not fit the social stereotype for appropriate female behavior (i.e., marrying and raising a family). Women who are diagnosed as having a dependent personality disorder may be so diagnosed because they represent exaggerations of gender role stereotypes (i.e., women should be dependent but not too dependent). Clearly, women who kill their children do not fit the social stereotypes for mothers or women and may receive a diagnosis on that basis. So we present our hypotheses with great caution.

40. P. T. d'Orban, "Women Who Kill Their Children," *British Journal of Psychiatry* 134 (1979): 562.

41. Dominique Bourget and John M. W. Bradford, "Homicidal Parents," *Canadian Journal of Psychiatry* 35 (1990): 235.

NOTES TO CHAPTER 4

1. Peggy McIntosh, "White Privilege: Unpacking the Invisible Knapsack," in *Re-Visioning Family Therapy: Race, Culture, and Gender in Clinical Practice*, ed. M. M. McGoldrick (New York: Guilford Press, 1998).

2. McIntosh, "White Privilege," 148.

3. Jean Baker Miller, "Women and Power," in *Women's Growth in Connection: Writings from the Stone Center*, ed. J. V. Jordan, A. G. Kaplan, J. B. Miller, I. P. Stiver, and J. L. Surrey (New York: Guilford Press, 1991), 198.

4. Elaine Pinderhughes, *Understanding Race, Ethnicity, and Power: The Key to Efficacy in Clinical Practice* (New York: Free Press, 1989), 109–110.

5. U.S. Department of Health and Human Services, Administration on Children, Youth and Families, Child Maltreatment 1998: Reports from the States to the National Child Abuse and Neglect Data System (Washington, D.C.: U.S. Government Printing Office, 2000).

6. *Child Maltreatment 1998: Reports:* "Findings required by the Child Abuse Prevention and Treatment Act, as amended in 1996, to be included in

all annual State data reports to the Secretary of Health and Human Services. Because this is only the second year that many of these data have been required, not all states were able to provide data on every item."

7. *Child Maltreatment 1998: Reports.*

8. Federal Interagency Forum on Child and Family Statistics, America's Children: Key National Indicators of Child Well-Being 2000 (Washington, D.C.: U.S. Government Printing Office, 2000), 6.

9. Federal Interagency Forum, *Child Well-Being 2000.*

10. In one study the circumstances surrounding insufficient supervision were examined. Parents reported that they left their children unsupervised because they were working, "taking care of something," socializing, out being entertained, involved in alcohol and/or drug-related activity, or sleeping. Approximately 50 percent of case records in the study included the parent's explanation. Of these cases, 40 percent stated that nothing was wrong with their neglectful behavior, and 22 percent stated they "had no choice" but to leave the children unattended. In several cases, parents stated that the substitute caregiver, typically the oldest child in the home, was mature enough to take care of younger children, or that the child knew how to contact the mother or a neighbor if any problems arose. M. Jones, *Parental Lack of Supervision: Nature and Consequences of a Major Child Neglect Problem* (Washington, D.C.: Child Welfare League of America, 1987).

11. One case that was excluded involved a mother whose child was killed in a car crash. No one riding in the vehicle was wearing a safety belt, and subsequently the police held the mother responsible for the child's death. There are likely many other cases which fit this pattern but they did not appear in our searches.

12. James M. Gaudin, *Child Neglect: A Guide for Intervention* (Washington, D.C.: United States Department of Health and Human Services, National Center on Child Abuse and Neglect, 1993), 17.

13. S. J. Bishop and B. J. Leadbeater, "Maternal Social Support Patterns and Child Maltreatment: Comparison of Maltreating and Nonmaltreating Mothers," *American Journal of Orthopsychiatry* 69 (April 1999): 172–181.

14. Bishop and Leadbeater, "Maternal Social Support Patterns"; J. M. Gaudin, "Effective Intervention with Neglectful Families," *Criminal Justice and Behavior* 20 (1993): 66–89.

15. R. A. Thompson, *Preventing Child Maltreatment Through Social Support: A Critical Analysis* (Thousand Oaks, Ca: Sage, 1995).

16. Gaudin, "Effective Intervention."

17. Robert M. Brayden, William A. Altemeir, Dorothy D. Tucker, Mary S. Dietrich, and Peter Vietze, "Antecedents of Child Neglect in the First Two Years of Life," *Journal of Pediatrics* 120 (1992): 426–429.

18. Federal Interagency Forum, 50.

19. *DSM-IV* reports: "The lifetime risk for Major Depressive Disorder in community samples has varied from 10% to 25% for women and from 5% to 12% for men." (pg. 341). American Psychiatric Association, *Diagnostic and Statistical Manual of Mental Disorders,* 4th ed. (Washington, D.C.: American Psychiatric Association, 1994), 341.

20. E. Milling Kinard, "Social Support, Competence and Depression in Mothers of Abused Children," *American Journal of Orthopsychiatry* 66 (1996): 460.

21. Staff Writer, "Mom Guilty in Starving Death of Toddler," *San Diego Union Tribune,* October 8, 1999, B10.

22. Richard J. Gelles, "Policy Issues in Child Neglect," in *Neglected Children: Research, Practice and Policy*, ed. H. Dubowitz (Thousand Oaks, Calif.: Sage, 1999), 284.

23. M. Chaffin, K. Kelleher, and J. Hollenberg, "Onset of Physical Abuse and Neglect: Psychiatric, Substance Abuse and Social Risk Factors from Prospective Community Data," *Child Abuse and Neglect* 20 (1996): 191–203.

24. Kathy Scruggs, "Baby Choked on Cockroach, Autopsy Finds; City Neglected Infested Apartment, Family Says," *Atlanta Journal Constitution,* May 26, 1996, 01G.

25. Beth Powell, "A Legacy of Loved Ones," *Atlanta Journal Constitution,* June 2, 1996, Editorial, 07C.

26. Mark R. Rank, "Access to Justice: The Racial Injustice of Poverty," *Washington University Journal of Law and Policy* 95 (1999): 2.

27. Veronica D. Abney, "Cultural Competency in the Field of Child Maltreatment," in *The APSAC Handbook on Child Maltreatment*, ed. J. Briere et al. (Thousand Oaks, Calif.: Sage, 1996).

28. Abney, "Cultural Competency"; see also Chaffin, Kelleher, and Hollenberg, "Onset of Physical Abuse and Neglect," 191–203.

29. A full history, mission, and philosophy of the Healthy Steps model can be obtained at HYPERLINK "http://www.healthysteps.org.www.healthysteps.org.

30. The term "Healthy Steps Specialists" has been coined by the Healthy Steps for Young Children Program.

31. Miller, "Women and Power," 205.

NOTES TO CHAPTER 5

1. Joe Sexton, "Mother of Elisa Izquierdo Pleads Guilty to Murder in a Pivotal Child-Abuse Case," *New York Times*, June 25, 1996, Late Edition.

2. As cited in Joel S. Milner, K. R. Robertson, and D. L. Rogers, "Childhood History of Abuse and Adult Child Abuse Potential," *Journal of Family Violence* 5 (1990): 15–34.

3. D. Cicchetti, "How Research on Child Maltreatment Has Informed the Study of Child Development: Perspectives from Developmental Psychopathology," in *Child Maltreatment: Theory and Research on the Causes and Consequences of Child Abuse and Neglect,* ed. D. Cicchetti and V. Carlson (New York: Cambridge University Press, 1989), 377–431. As cited in Lynne A. Hall, Barbara Sachs, and Mary Kay Rayens, "Mothers' Potential for Child Abuse: The Roles of Childhood Abuse and Social Resources," *Nursing Research* 47 (March/April 1998): 87–95.

4. Bong Joo Lee and Robert M. George, "Poverty, Early Childbearing and Child Maltreatment: A Multinominal Analysis," *Children and Youth Services Report* 21 (September–October 1999): 755–780.

5. J. de Paul and L. Domenech, "Childhood History of Abuse and Child Abuse Potential in Adolescent Mothers: A Longitudinal Study," *Child Abuse and Neglect* 25 (May 2000): 701–713.

6. K. D. Jennings, S. Ross, S. Popper, and M. Elmore, "Thoughts of Harming Infants in Depressed and Nondepressed Mothers," *Journal of Affective Disorders* 54 (July 1999): 21–28.

7. E. Milling Kinard, "Social Support, Competence, and Depression in Mothers of Abused Children," *American Journal of Orthopsychiatry* 66 (July 1996): 449–462. See also Sandra J. Bishop and Bonnie J. Leadbeater, "Maternal Social Support Patterns and Child Maltreatment: Comparison of Mal-

treating and Nonmaltreating Mothers," *American Journal of Orthopsychiatry* 69 (April 1999): 172–181.

8. Bishop and Leadbeater, "Maternal Social Support."

9. Martha Smithey, "Infant Homicide at the Hands of Mothers: Toward a Sociological Perspective," *Deviant Behavior: An Interdisciplinary Journal* 18 (1997): 255–272.

10. Susan J. Kelley, "Stress and Coping Behaviors of Substance-Abusing Mothers," *Journal of the Society of Pediatric Nurses* 3 (July–September 1998): 103–110.

11. B. A. Miller, N. J. Smith, and P. J. Mudar, "Mothers' Alcohol and Other Drug Problems and Their Punitiveness toward Children," *Journal of Studies on Alcohol* 60 (September 1999): 632–642.

12. Carol Coohey and Norman Braun, "Toward an Integrated Framework for Understanding Child Physical Abuse," *Child Abuse and Neglect* 21 (November 1997): 1081–1094.

13. Hall, Sachs, and Rayens, "Mothers' Potential."

14. Philip J. Resnick, "Child Murder by Parents: A Psychiatric Review of Filicide," *American Journal of Psychiatry*, 126 (September 1969): 325–334.

15. Resnick, "Child Murder."

16. Dominique Bourget and John M. W. Bradford, "Homicidal Parents," *Canadian Journal of Psychiatry* 35 (April 1990): 233–238.

17. P. T. d'Orban, "Women Who Kill Their Children," *British Journal of Psychiatry* 134 (1979): 560–571.

18. Christine M. Alder and June Baker, "Maternal Filicide: More Than One Story to Be Told," *Women and Criminal Justice* 9 (1997): 15–39.

19. Ania Wilczynski, *Child Homicide* (New York: Oxford University Press, 1997).

20. Hillary Rodham Clinton, in her book, *It Takes a Village,* stated that "we should be willing to terminate parental rights more quickly whenever physical or sexual abuse is involved." Hillary Rodham Clinton, *It Takes a Village and Other Lessons Children Teach Us* (New York: Simon and Schuster, 1996), 49.

21. Child Abuse Prevention and Treatment Act, Public Law 93-247 (1974).

22. However, this creates new problems because it is up to judicial

discretion to decide whether a case warrants nondisclosure and there are no guidelines. Bazelton outlines a set of factors which should be considered when making disclosure decisions including the child's age, maturity, type of proceeding, and the child's wishes. Emily Bazelton, "Public Access to Juvenile and Family Court: Should the Courtroom Doors Be Open or Closed?" *Yale Law and Policy Review* 18 (1999): 155.

23. Child Abuse Prevention and Treatment Act, as amended, *U.S. Code,* vol. 42, sec. 5106a (1996).

24. William Wesley Patton, "Pandora's Box: Opening Child Protection Cases to the Press and the Public," *Western State University Law Review* 27 (1999/2000): 181.

25. Adoption Assistance and Child Welfare Act of 1980, *U.S. Code Annotated*, vol. 42, sec. 620–628.

26. Some states set reunification limits at six months, others at twelve months.

27. Adoption and Safe Families Act of 1997, *U.S. Code,* vol. 42, sec. 1305.

28. Kathleen A. Bailie, "The Other 'Neglected' Parties in Child Protective Proceedings: Parents in Poverty and the Role of the Lawyers Who Represent Them," *Fordham Law Review* 66 (May 1998): 2285.

29. Jill Sheldon, "50,000 Children Are Waiting: Permanency, Planning and Termination of Parental Rights under the Adoption Assistance and Child Welfare Act of 1980," *Boston College Third World Law Review* 17 (Winter 1997): 73.

30. Sheldon, "50,000 Children."

31. However, turning services over to private agencies has problems too, including the state's inability to monitor private agencies, thus providing more opportunity for misspending and a general lack of monitoring.

32. There are many thoughtful analyses of transracial adoption. For example, see Suzanne Brannen Campbell, "Taking Race out of the Equation: Transracial Adoption in 2000," *Southern Methodist Law Review* 53: 1599. Campbell discusses the National Association of Black Social Workers position paper and the impact (or lack thereof) of recent legislation such as the Multi-Ethnic Placement Act and amendments to it.

33. Timothy Roche, "The Crisis of Foster Care," *Time* 156 (November 13,

2000): 74–82; see also James Rainey, "Foster Child Adoptions Soar in California," *Los Angeles Times,* May 8, 2000, A1.

34. Roche, "The Crisis of Foster Care."

35. Roche, "The Crisis of Foster Care."

36. Nina Bernstein and Frank Bruni, "Seven Warnings: A Special Report; She Suffered in Plain Sight But Alarms Were Ignored," *New York Times*, December 24, 1995, Late Edition.

37. Bernstein and Bruni, "Seven Warnings."

38. Bob Port, "Reform after Tragedy: Girl's Death Shook Up City," *Daily News* (New York), November 20, 2000, Sports Final Edition.

39. Joyce Purnick, "Elisa's Death: A Year Later, Hints of Hope," *New York Times*, November 21, 1996, Late Edition. It is interesting to note that in order to balance the budget, Mayor Giuliani had cut the city's child welfare funding several years before Elisa died.

40. Lizette Alvarez, "Report in Wake of Girl's Death Finds Failure in Child Agency," *New York Times*, April 9, 1996, Late Edition.

41. Corky Siemaszko, "Haunting Reminder of Elisa," *Daily News* (New York), September 2, 1996.

42. Alvarez, "Report in Wake."

43. This was revealed during an audit in which random interviews were conducted with Administration for Children's Services staff. Port, "Reform after Tragedy."

44. Purnick, "Elisa's Death."

45. "Three More Promises to Keep," *Daily News* (New York), December 1, 1997, Editorial.

46. "Three More Promises to Keep."

47. Kathleen A. Bailie, "The Other."

48. Roche, "The Crisis of Foster Care."

49. Wendy Hundley, "Past Abusers Targeted," *Dayton Daily News*, October 12, 1996, City Edition; Wendy Hundley, "Ruling: Boy, 2, Slain," *Dayton Daily News*, October 4, 1996, City Edition.

50. Wendy Hundley, "New Protections for Kids," *Dayton Daily News*, December 7, 1996, City Edition.

51. "Family or Village," *Christian Science Monitor*, September 17, 1996, Editorial.

52. "Family or Village."

53. Roche, "The Crisis of Foster Care."

54. Port, "Reform after Tragedy."

55. Dennis Chaptman, "Child Abuse Bill Proposes Monitoring Protection: Measure Allows Volunteers to Watch, Interview Victims; Opponent Calls It Intrusive," *Milwaukee Journal Sentinel*, December 1, 1999; "'Drake London Bill' Goes to Governor for Signing," Associated Press, March 22, 2000.

56. Roche, "The Crisis of Foster Care."

57. Brid Featherstone, "Victims or Villains? Women Who Physically Abuse Their Children," in *Violence and Gender Relations: Theories and Interventions,* ed. Barbara Fawcett and Brid Featherstone (London: Sage, 1996), 178–189.

NOTES TO CHAPTER 6

1. Rosalind Bentley and H. J. Cummins, "Poverty, Despair, Illness Often Found in Mothers Who Kill: A 1995 'Profile' of Mothers Who Murder Their Children Found They Often Share a Deadly Medley of Life Stressors," *Star Tribune*, September 5, 1998, 18A.

2. Patrick J. Resnick, "Murder of the Newborn: A Psychiatric Review of Neonaticide," *American Journal of Psychiatry* 126 (1970): 1414–1420.

3. Lenore E. Walker, *The Battered Woman* (New York: HarperPerennial, 1979).

4. Ola W. Barnett and Alyce D. LaViolette, *It Could Happen to Anyone: Why Battered Women Stay* (Newbury Park, Calif.: Sage, 1993).

5. Walker, *The Battered Woman.*

6. Barnett and LaViolette, *It Could Happen.*

7. J. A. Mercy and L. E. Saltzman, "Fatal Violence among Spouses in the United States, 1976–1985," *American Journal of Public Health* 79 (1989): 595–599.

8. A. Toufexis, "Home Is Where the Hurt Is: Wife Beating among the Well-to-Do No Longer a Secret," *Time* (December 21, 1987): 68.

9. Federal Bureau of Investigation (FBI), "Uniform Crime Reports for the United States" (Washington, D.C.: Government Printing Office, 1989).

10. Susan Murphy-Milano, *Defending Our Lives: Getting Away from Domestic Violence and Staying Safe* (New York: Doubleday, 1996).

11. R. H. C. Teske, Jr. and M. L. Parker, "Spouse Abuse in Texas: A Study of Women's Attitudes and Experiences," Criminal Justice Center, Survey Research Program (1983).

12. Ginny NiCarthy, *Getting Free: You Can End Abuse and Take Back Your Life* (Seattle: Seal Press, 1982).

13. Barnett and LaViolette, *It Could Happen*.

14. NiCarthy, *Getting Free*.

15. Walker, *The Battered Woman*.

16. Walker, *The Battered Woman*.

17. Barnett and LaViolette, *It Could Happen*.

18. Murphy-Milano, *Defending Our Lives;* and NiCarthy, *Getting Free*.

19. Barnett and LaViolette, *It Could Happen*.

20. Amy R. Melner, "Rights of Abused Mothers versus Best Interest of Abused Children: Courts' Termination of Battered Women's Parental Rights Due to Failure to Protect Their Children from Abuse," *Southern California Review of Law and Women's Studies* 7 (1998): 299.

21. Susan Brewster, *To Be an Anchor in the Storm: A Guide for Families and Friends of Abused Women* (New York: Ballantine Books, 1997).

22. Murphy-Milano, *Defending Our Lives*.

23. Barnett and LaViolette, *It Could Happen;* and Walker, *The Battered Woman*.

24. Barnett and LaViolette, *It Could Happen*.

25. Lesley E. Daigle, "Empowering Women to Protect: Improving Intervention with Victims of Domestic Violence in Cases of Child Abuse and Neglect: A Study of Travis County, Texas," *Texas Journal of Women and the Law* 7 (1998): 287.

26. Mary D. Overpeck, Ruth A. Brenner, Ann C. Trumble, Lara B. Trifiletti, and Heinz W. Berendes, "Risk Factors for Infant Homicide in the United States," *New England Journal of Medicine* 339 (October 1998): 1211–1216.

27. Martha Woodall, "When Mom's Boyfriend Turns Killer," *Philadelphia Inquirer*, August 20, 1995, A1.

28. Melner, "Rights of Abused Mothers."

29. George A. Gellert, Roberta M. Maxwell, Michael J. Durfee, and Gerald A. Wagner, "Fatalities Assessed by the Orange County Child Death Review Team, 1989 to 1991," *Child Abuse and Neglect* 19 (1995): 875–883.

30. Martha Smithey, "Infant Homicide: Victim/Offender Relationship and Causes of Death," *Journal of Family Violence* 13 (1998): 285–297.

31. Walker, *The Battered Woman.*

32. Walker, *The Battered Woman.*

33. Barnett and LaViolette, *It Could Happen.*

34. Cheryl L. Meyer, Tara C. Proano, and James R. Franz, "Postpartum Syndromes: Disparate Treatment in the Legal System," in *It's a Crime: Women and Justice,* ed. Roslyn Muraskin (Upper Saddle River, N.J.: Prentice Hall, 2000).

35. Barnett and LaViolette, *It Could Happen.*

36. Walker, *The Battered Woman.*

37. Eric Nagourney, "Defense in Baby-Killing: Woman Will Claim Husband Buried Infant," *Newsday,* February 5, 1994, 11.

38. "Murder Convictions Upheld, Despite Presence of Judge's Wife on Jury," *Chicago Daily Law Bulletin,* November 19, 1992, 3.

39. Meyer, Proano, and Franz, "Postpartum Syndromes."

40. Meyer, Proano, and Franz, "Postpartum Syndromes."

41. Michelle Oberman, "Mothers Who Kill: Coming to Terms with Modern American Infanticide," *American Criminal Law Review* 34 (1996): 1–108.

42. Michelle S. Jacobs, "Criminal Law: Requiring Battered Women Die: Murder Liability for Mothers under Failure to Protect Statutes," *Northwestern School of Law Journal of Criminal Law and Criminology* (Winter 1998): 578.

43. Jacobs, "Criminal Law."

44. Melner, "Rights of Abused Mothers."

45. Melner, "Rights of Abused Mothers."

46. Melner, "Rights of Abused Mothers."

47. Carol Marbin Miller, "Abuse Cases Prompt Parenting Skills Program," *St. Petersburg Times,* January 24, 1998, 4B.

NOTES TO CHAPTER 7

1. Linda Chavez, "The Tragic Story of Medea Still Lives," *Denver Post,* December 3, 1995, E04.

2. Chavez, "Tragic Story."

3. Lynn Smith, "Experts Seek Reasons Behind Irrational Crime," *Los Angeles Times*, October 15, 1991, A25.

4. See K. Chew, R. McCleary, M. Lew, and J. Wang, "Epidemiology of Child Homicide: California, 1981–1990," *Homicide Studies* 2 (1999): 78–85.

5. Chew et al., "Epidemiology."

6. 1938 1 and 2 Geo. VII, c. 36 (Eng.).

7. Nigel Walker, *Crime and Insanity in England,* vol. 1 (Edinburgh: Edinburgh University Press, 1973), 133.

8. See, e.g., Judith A. Osborne, "The Crime of Infanticide: Throwing Out the Baby with the Bathwater," *Canadian Review of Family Law* 6 (1987): 47, 55; see also Walker, *Crime and Insanity,* 128, in which Walker describes the difficulties of fashioning an alternative legal approach to infanticide.

9. Like most trial court decisions, Ms. Gindorf's original conviction is not reported. Her appeal, which she lost, is reported in *People v. Gindorf,* 159 Ill. App. 3d 647, 512 N.E. 2d 770 (1987).

10. See chapter 3 on purposeful killing.

11. Susan Smith was sentenced to thirty-eight years in prison for killing her two sons.

12. Don Thompson, "Death Penalty Politics Fail to Solve Question of How to Ensure Justice," *Chicago Daily Herald*, February 6, 2000, 1.

13. Michael Perlin calls infanticide defendants "empathy outliers," noting that "juries have appeared to be inordinately (and perhaps, even inappropriately) sympathetic" in judging them. See Michael L. Perlin, *The Jurisprudence of the Insanity Defense* (Durham, N.C.: Carolina Press, 1994), 192. See also Janan Hanna and Art Barnum, "Prosecutors to Seek Death Penalty for Lemak," *Chicago Tribune,* Febrary 3, 2000, 1, noting the political considerations surrounding the decision to seek the death penalty, and the fact that juries tend not to sentence women to death.

14. Rob Modic, "Jury Convicts Nobles in Drowning of Son," *Dayton Daily News*, February 12, 1994, 1A.

15. Modic, "Jury Convicts."

16. See Kevin Lamb, "Trial Touched on Some Emotional Issues," *Dayton Daily News*, June 23, 1995, B1, for a description of these tensions.

17. Lamb, "Trial Touched." Lamb notes that a common refrain following

every procedural decision leading up to the case's ultimate resolution was: "Why was she different from Tanisha Nobles, the black woman who was convicted in 1994 of killing her 2-year-old son, Erick?"

18. Wes Hills, "Judge Sends Teen to Adult System; Hopfer Case Goes to Grand Jury," *Dayton Daily News*, November 18, 1994, A1.

19. Lamb, "Trial Touched."

20. See, e.g., Michael A. Scott, "Letter to the Editor," *Dayton Daily News*, July 17, 1995, A6: "There have been several cases right here in the Miami Valley in which young mothers have been accused and convicted of killing their children. . . . Why is it that these girls were not afforded the same special treatment as Hopfer? . . . Could it be because her parents have influence and money? Could it be because Hopfer is white?"

21. Indeed, it did not stop with the trial, but continued as Hopfer's case wound its way through the appellate courts. Local newspapers continued to receive letters such as the following:

It's too bad that Brenda K. Hopfer thinks her daughter was convicted to appease the black community. It seems to me that people of any color would be interested in seeing justice served even-handedly. If Rebecca Hopfer gets freed, then authorities should free . . . Tanisha Nobles or any other mother who's in prison for the death of her children.

Dayton Daily News, "Speak Up!" Op-ed page, February 27, 1998, 17A.

22. For a set of proposed statues designed to harmonize U.S. treatment of infanticide cases, see Michelle Oberman, "Mothers Who Kill: Coming to Terms with Modern American Infanticide," *American Criminal Law Review* 34 (1996): 77–88.

23. Although there has not yet been a comparative study of British and U.S. infanticide rates, the many works on the subject by British scholars suggest very steady rates of infanticide, and reveal no problem with recidivism among those convicted and sentenced to probation. See, for example, Ania Wilczynski, "Images of Women Who Kill Their Infants: The Mad and the Bad," *Women and Criminal Justice* 2 (1991): 71–73; Susan M. Edwards, "Neither Mad nor Bad: The Female Violent Offender Reassessed," *Women's Studies International Forum* 9 (1986): 79.

24. See William L. Langer, "Infanticide: A Historical Survey," 1 *History of Childhood Quarterly* (1974): 353–354.

25. Consider, for example, the history of foundling homes, offered in Rachel G. Fuchs's *Poor and Pregnant in Paris: Strategies for Survival in the Nineteenth Century* (Piscataway: Rutgers University Press, 1992). In this book, Fuchs notes that these homes, found throughout most large European towns in that era, were overwhelmed with infants. As the number of children abandoned at the homes exceeded the homes' capacity to care for them, the governments turned instead to programs designed to provide outside aid to unwed mothers. See also Langer, "Infanticide," 359.

INDEX

ABOUT THE AUTHORS

Cheryl L. Meyer is Associate Professor at the School of Professional Psychology at Wright State University, and the author of *The Wandering Uterus: Politics and the Reproductive Rights of Women*.

Michelle Oberman is Professor in the College of Law at DePaul University, and teaches and lectures at various Chicago area hospitals. She has written numerous articles about women, sexuality, and the law.

Kelly White is a doctoral candidate in clinical psychology at Wright State University School of Professional Psychology.

Michelle Rone is a doctoral candidate in clinical psychology at Wright State University School of Professional Psychology.

Priya Batra is currently completing her postdoctoral fellowship in clinical psychology at Dartmouth-Hitchcock Medical Center in New Hampshire.

Tara C. Proano is completing a postdoctoral internship in the area of health psychology at the University of Colorado Health Sciences Center in Denver, Colorado.